# BRANDON
## a prospect of a city

Before parking and traffic restrictions on Rosser

East side of Tenth Street, looking south, ca. 1911

# BRANDON
# a prospect of a city

A project of
the Brandon Division Association
Manitoba Teachers' Society

Mary Hume, Editor

Published by the City of Brandon

Making corn silage at the Experimental Farm, ca. 1900

Printed by
Leech Printing Ltd.
Brandon, Manitoba, Canada
1981

ISBN 0-920436-07-2

Second Printing — 1982

# Introduction

In planning the celebration of our city's centenary the Brandon Centennial Committee decided some two years ago to go to the people for suggestions as to what forms the celebrations might take. "Let's have a pictorial history. Get the old photographs out of the albums and the archival collections into a book we can all have in our homes," was in essence one of the prevailing messages. This book is offered in response to that suggestion.

Of course, the whole story cannot be told in pictures alone, for the camera is not always on the ready when important events take place. Nor are all the photographs that are necessary to tell the story accessible — some are still hidden in old albums and shoeboxes.

The selection of photos in this book came from many sources, and not a few were taken by amateur photographers. Some pictures record occasions that many will recall, but the greater number tell of times in the Brandon of another day well beyond the recollection of people living today. They show us a little of how our city has grown, as well as something of life in the rural area surrounding the city.

Brandon has most generally been known as *The Wheat City*. In brochures, in newspaper and magazine articles written about this city, we have been called other names as well. We have chosen to use a few of the bynames as section titles, and we have arranged the four hundred or so photographs as we felt they fit into a particular section. Some effort has been made as well to observe a chronological order where possible.

In choosing a title for the book we felt that the logo adopted for the Centennial suggested that we were attempting to do — to present a view, a prospect, of our city. From where we stand as the city's first century turns to the next, we catch a glimpse of those events that have helped make the city what it is.

The very brief history written by Tom Mitchell as a prologue to the pictorial record, and the explanatory notes with the pictures are offered as well to enhance the view of our city.

We invite you, then, to look at the city as it appeared in the camera lens of an earlier day. Any association you can make with the subject of a photograph can help bridge the years, and so heighten your appreciation of our city as it is today.

The city is growing still, and many who today look at these records of the past will have a share in building to-morrow's future.

An experiment in flight, ca. 1925

# Contents

A quiet Brandon street, ca. 1920

# Prologue

"Confederation . . . [had been] brought about to realize the commercial potentialities of the St. Lawrence . . . ." The policies pursued by the Conservative government of John A. Macdonald in laying the basis for western expansion were conceived and acted upon with a view primarily to the interests of central Canada. The West, after being settled, was to be a reservoir of natural resources and agricultural produce and a market for the tariff-protected manufactured goods of eastern Canada. East and West were to be tied together with a ribbon of iron.

It is in this historical context that one must view the birth of Brandon and the events which called into being the Wheat City as a regional trading, distribution, service, and transportation centre on this river of iron which was to tie the West to the commercial empire of the St. Lawrence and the world beyond.

Following the acquisition of the Northwest from the Hudson's Bay Company in 1869 and, in 1870, the creation of the postage stamp province of Manitoba — Riel's bequest to an ungrateful nation — the federal government instituted a number of measures to promote the settlement of the West. Federal control over the lands and natural resources of the Northwest was legislated to expedite immigration, settlement, and railway construction. Aboriginal title to the lands was nullified by treaties agreed to by Indian leaders and government officials in the 1870's. The North West Mounted Police, created and sent west in 1873, were to signal Canadian sovereignty in the Northwest and ensure orderly, lawful settlement. A survey of the West was begun in 1869. The Winnipeg Meridian was selected as a base line and the section of 640 acres the basic unit. In 1872 The Dominion Lands Act was passed, under which a settler could obtain a quarter-section of 160 acres for a ten dollar registration fee, title to the land to be gained in three years provided settlement duties were fulfilled. The settler could also secure preemption rights to a neighbouring quarter-section.

Brandon skyline from the other side of the tracks, ca. 1913

In 1881 Parliament enlarged the province by moving the western boundary to its present location and the northern boundary to 53° latitude; the site of the future city of Brandon was henceforth within Manitoba. Efforts to construct a transcontinental railway, which finally bore fruit with the creation of the Canadian Pacific Railway on October 21, 1880, completed the series of actions taken to ensure that the Northwest assumed its role in John A. Macdonald's vision of the Kingdom of Canada.

In May, 1881 General T.L. Rosser, American Civil War veteran and engineer for the Canadian Pacific Railway Company, selected a site on the south side of the Assiniboine River two miles west of the recently-established Grand Valley settlement as a divisional point on the railway. Here water tanks, loading platforms, warehouses, elevators, and stations would be erected to nourish the iron python that was making its way westward. Here as well would be located the first city in the Northwest, summoned into being by the CPR as a transportation, service, and trading centre for the agricultural hinterland that surrounded it. On October 11, 1881 the first Canadian Pacific passenger train clattered across the Assiniboine and by May 30, 1882 the "Wonder City of the Northwest", the City of Brandon, was a reality in fact and in law.

It had been a dramatic twelve months, containing as it did Rosser's sudden appearance on the spring-green slopes of the Assiniboine; his abrupt rejection of the Grand Valley site; the arrival of waves of settlers — 1,500 a week — by foot, horse, steamboat, and rail; and the frenzied transformation, after the arrival of Whitehead and Myer with their lumber, of a huddle of tents into rough-hewn wooden business establishments and residences. There had been feverish inflation and wild speculation in land; one Nova Scotian made $200,000 in land deals. Public meetings were held to give formal direction and structure to the affairs of the new community. James A. Smart, one of the original settlers and later Mayor of Brandon, ventured that "No small town in Canada or elsewhere could possibly have contained a happier army of young men than did Brandon in its earliest days."

Cross-section of Brandon business community, May, 1882

The Brandon of the 1880's was an outpost of Ontario, connected with the outside world by rail and telegraph line. WASP-ish in culture and institutions, practical and pragmatic in outlook, the population was predominantly and unrepentingly Ontario- or British-born. Brandon's fourth estate surfaced when the *Brandon Sun* first hit the street on January 19, 1882. Professionals and businessmen proffered an array of services to the denizens of town and surrounding countryside. Weary labourers returned home slack-jawed at end of day after turning out cigars, tents, beer, sewer pipe, windmills, bricks, fire engines, or buggies at one of the thirty-nine manufacturing establishments. The women of the town conformed to the nineteenth-century role of matron of hearth and kin. C.E. Leigh, a young recruit passing through Brandon en route to the Saskatchewan Rebellion, wrote a tribute to them:

"Oh! the belles of Brandon
    Who cheered us on our way.
We'll not forget their kindness
    For many and many a day."

Inevitably, as in the early years of any frontier town, there were also more than a few *filles des nuits*. Land sharks and gamblers completed the cast.

Brick-making plant — where the building boom begins

The social life in Brandon prior to the turn of the century centred on home, school, and church. It also included a number of strenuous diversions. Curling, hockey, lacrosse, snowshoeing, and skating occupied many winter hours while summer brought a return to baseball, roller skating, bicycle rides, horse races, fairs, and picnics at Lake Clementi. Doubtless, many hours of sociable discourse occurred in one of the twenty-two hotels, most with liquor licenses, or on the even then ubiquitous telephone.

On the evening of July 3, 1882 T. Mayne Daly, Brandon's ebullient Mayor-elect, and twelve freshly-elected aldermen convened to hold Brandon City Council's inaugural meeting. The meeting took place in the Tenth Street school, which had only recently been constructed — and still stands — under the auspices of Chairman Dr. Alex Fleming and other members of Brandon's first School Board. The Council was all male and was to continue so until the election of Mrs. Rhoda Tennant in 1935. Like its successors, the first Council was drawn from the ranks of the business and professional community.

The Robert Lanes host a family picnic at Lake Clementi, 1903

One of Council's initial actions was to decree the immediate construction of civic offices, council chambers, a firehall, and a jail. It was here that Brandon was first exposed to the rigours of capital punishment when one William Webb was hanged at 8:15 a.m. on December 28, 1888 for the murder of his wife. Our first courthouse, erected in 1883 with debentures issued by The County of Brandon, later became the Provincial Gaol.

Council was kept afoot during the decade making provision for public health, education, street lights (which were electric by 1889), and the grading of Rosser Avenue and Sixth Street. These two by-ways had emerged as the main business arteries in the city. Council also acquired ownership of the First and Eighteenth Street bridges which had had strife-filled histories as toll bridges since their construction early in the decade.

Allied with the exertions of Council to provide Brandonites with the amenities of urban life were the efforts of Henry L. Patmore, later Alderman Patmore, who in 1889 embarked on his personal crusade to beautify the city. In later years, the shady, tree-clad streets encouraged the view that the city of Brandon was "undoubtedly the most beautiful in the Canadian Northwest".

Brandon's first Civic Offices. See Plan.

| Seventh Street | | | |
|---|---|---|---|
| Downstairs was the fire engine room | Dan M McMillan Treasurer's Office upstairs on west. Stairs from Ground Floor | Council Chamber for city--upstairs, west side. Underneath was Police Station and Chief of Police Office on west side | Police Court on east side underneath was the prisoner cell |
| Princess Avenue | John C Kerr's Office City Clerk upstairs on east. | | |
| | Hose Tower | A R Crawford's house at rear | |
| Door to Hose House | Hose Reel House and Horse Stable | Upstairs Volunteer brigade met and hostlers slept | |
| Door to Horse Stables. | This is frame building with stairs | | |
| | Land Titles Registrar's Office    Martin MacDonald | | |
| Lane | | | |

Plan of Brandon's first Fire Hall, 1882-1911, and Civic Offices, 1882-1892.
(Present City Hall built 1892. Present Fire Hall built 1911.)

Brandon City Hall Complex, 1882 - 1892

Brandon emerged in the 1880's as a focus of economic and political leadership in the southwest region of Manitoba. Here on December 5, 1883 the Farmers' Protective Union of Manitoba was created. Early in the new century Brandon would be the setting for the formation of the Manitoba Grain Growers' Association. Brandon also assumed the mantle of agricultural capital of Manitoba when the Federal Department of Agriculture created the Brandon Experimental Farm in 1886 by which date six elevators had been constructed along Pacific Avenue. Ironically, Brandon's role as the principal market centre for southwestern Manitoba led, in 1887 with the wheat blockade of that year, to Brandon's being crowned with the sobriquet of "The Wheat City".

Characteristically, Brandon did not stand still in the 1890's. The central business district was rebuilt after a disastrous fire in 1889. Brandon Academy, soon to be Brandon College, was created in 1890. Central School and the new Brandon Hospital opened in 1892, while in 1893 the municipally-owned waterworks was inaugurated.

In 1897 A.E. McKenzie's seed company was founded. Its far-flung trade gave credence to the assertion that Brandon was more than just a typical small, rural market centre and railway town of 5,000 souls. If further evidence was needed, Brandonites could point to the fact that by 1900 Brandon was the eastern terminus of the Great North West Central, the western terminus of the Northern Pacific Railway, and a major divisional point on the Canadian Pacific.

While these developments transformed the original site of Brandon, Canada was emerging not as a vital, growing young nation but appeared more in the guise of "a huge demographic railway station". In the years from 1882 to 1891 Brandon's population increased from 700 to 3,700. Yet in the same period Canada, while attracting some 1,256,000 immigrants, in fact lost 1,546,000 of its potential citizenry primarily to the United States.

The solution to the Canadian dilemma lay not in the development policies of Canadian governments following 1867, but in the basic nature of the western wheat economy and the economic conditions prevalent in the world. The most important factors for the successful development of the West were its commercial relations with the wheat markets of the world and its ability to grow and export its staple product, wheat. Production and sale of western Canadian wheat and the resulting influx of population to the West only became possible with the convergence of a number of developments around the year 1896.

Passage to Canada for two adults and two children, from England

Several of these developments had occurred prior to 1896. The climatic and topograhical conditions of the western plains had been known and deemed favourable to agricultural pursuits since the Hind and Palliser expeditions of 1857. By the early 1880's the required varieties of grain and techniques essential for the successful production had been developed. In 1881 the Canadian Pacific Railway and the Manitoba Agricultural Society provided and encouraged the use of Red Fife, a hard spring wheat, which was to become the standard wheat grown until the development of Marquis in 1912. The invention of roller milling in 1878 "had converted the hardness of spring wheat from a blemish to a virtue". Moreover, by the late 1870's the Mennonite settlers of Manitoba had introduced "dry farming", a combination of summer fallowing, irrigation, and the use of dugouts which were essential for successful farming on the western plains. This technique was later supplemented by the introduction of the mechanical drill, the chilled steel plow, the self-binding scooper, the steam thresher, and barbed wire, which collectively made large-scale agricultural operations possible.

The mechanization of grain elevators facilitating the storage and grading of grain also made its appearance in the 1880's. The completion of the Canadian Pacific Railway in 1885, combined with the development of the steel hull and the compound steam engine, and the deepening of the St. Lawrence canal system in the 1890's, provided a sure, safe, and most importantly, cheap transportation network to get the crop to market. These innovations in oceanic transport reduced the cost of shipping a bushel of wheat from Montreal to Liverpool from twenty cents in 1875 to two cents a bushel in 1904. The cost of rail transport remained constant during this period at around twenty cents a bushel.

Then, in 1896 the persistent economic malaise which had been a blight on the world economy waned. Investment capital, so necessary to fuel western development, became abundant. From the industrial cities of northwestern Europe came a seemingly insatiable demand for North American wheat. In the United States in 1896, agricultural settlement ebbed because of a growing shortage of good land at low cost. The Canadian West was now to become the terminus of the great human stream which had, until then, flowed on to the vast upland plains of the northwestern United States.

Stack threshing with power from the Dunbar Outfit's Case steamer, 1883

14

Change was in the air and, in Ottawa, the remnants of the Tory dynasty, which had ruled Canada for the previous eighteen years, were being moved aside to make way for the new Liberal government of Wilfrid Laurier. The new Member of Parliament from Brandon, Clifford Sifton, was named Minister of the Interior and given the task of directing the settlement of the sparsely populated Canadian West; James A. Smart, former Brandon mayor and MLA, was made Sifton's deputy minister. Sifton's appointment had come at a time when "events stronger than advocacy, even stronger than men" had appeared on the stage of Canadian and world affairs to hasten the settlement of the last extensive frontier for agricultural settlement in North America. The Canadian West was indeed the "Last Best West".

"There was a feeling of optimism in the air," reported the *Brandon Sun*. Everyone 'looked forward to a future that . . . [was] now pregnant with new life and bright hopes". The years of prosperity, which were to run their golden course until 1912, had at last appeared.

Honourable Clifford Sifton and Lady Sifton with sons Clifford, Jr., Harry, Winfield, John II, Victor

The most obvious effect on Brandon of these years of renewed western settlement and prosperity was the boost in its population from 5,000 in 1900 to 10,408 in 1906 and to 13,839 by 1911. Brandon's manufacturing productivity jumped three hundred percent in the same period. The year 1904, when 250 buildings were erected, was indicative of the construction boom during these years.

City Council extended and paved city streets; the waterworks was extended; and a beginning was made on a municipally-owned street railway system which was completed in 1913 and which continued in subsequent years to be a burden to municipal ratepayers. The stone and brick buildings in Brandon's central business district date from this period as do the stately homes which grace the central area of the city and bear testimony to the growing affluence of Brandon's Edwardian elite.

In Manitoba during the great western boom, urbanization was actually proceeding faster than rural settlement. Manitoba's sixteen percent growth in urban population during the years 1901 to 1911 was twice the national average. By 1911 forty-three percent of the province's population was urban, and with this development came the growth of labour and the Labour movement in the West. In Brandon, the largest section of voters by 1903 was comprised of working men. When the first Labour Day celebrations were held in the city in 1907, six unions were represented. In 1908 the CPR was the victim of a strike. The Brandon Trades and Labour Council was also active in the pre-war period, in particular calling for a public library, a municipally-owned telephone system, and a street railway. In Brandon it was increasingly clear that labour was a force to be reckoned with.

Paving on Ninth Street between Pacific and Rosser, 1910

While the growth of labour lent greater variation to the class structure of the community and sent school board officials off to design new curricula to meet the needs of industry, the population movements of the period also threatened to change the cultural character of the city. The influx of east-European population reduced the percentage of Brandonites of British lineage from eighty-three percent in 1901 to seventy-four percent in 1911. Victimized by autocracy in Europe and Anglo-Saxon ethnocentrism in Canada, the determination of the "men in sheepskin coats" to preserve their customs, language, and institutions resulted in not only a unique addition to Brandon's cityscape but also a community enriched socially and culturally by a people eager for opportunity, yet endlessly enduring, warm, and firm in friendship.

Brandon became famous across Canada during this period for its agricultural fairs, which began under the leadership of the indefatiguable J.D. McGregor in 1904. In 1913 Brandon held the Dominion Fair which continued for ten days and drew over 200,000 people.

Further renown was gained when Brandon defeated Rat Portage to qualify for play against Ottawa in the Stanley Cup final of 1904. Alas, Ottawa won; undoubtedly the effect of which to further delineate a nascent regional identity in southwestern Manitoba.

Ukrainian School with teacher Mr. Galan, at first National Home, built 1916, on Stickney Avenue

If interest in fairs or hockey waned, one could watch Charlie Chaplin, Stan Laurel, or The Keystone Cops at the Bijou, Starland, or Lyric theatres, established during the early 1900's.

In 1906 Brandon had become a terminus of the Great Northern, which provided a southward link to the St. Paul and Minneapolis Railway. In 1911 the Canadian Northern Railway selected Brandon as a divisional point between Winnipeg and Regina and began construction of the Prince Edward Hotel which, when completed, reflected the grace, elegance, and opulence of the period. The "Prince Eddy" was to become Brandon's most venerated architectural edifice, and opposition to its destruction in the late 1970's became a *cause célèbre*.

The western boom had been financed by pounds sterling, and when the Balkan Wars of 1912 and 1913 plunged Europe into World War I, the capital that had financed the construction of railway and elevators, towns and cities, and the purchase and equipping of farms, disappeared. The War began in August, 1914, but the boom had ended in 1912.

The Bijou, one of Brandon's six theatres in 1910

The city's population declined from 17,177 in 1914 to 14,012 in 1918. Many of those who left were heading east for military training and the European abattoir that was World War I.

The carnage of the war was mirrored at home on January 13, 1916 when a train wreck took the lives of seventeen Canadian Pacific Railway employees. Then on January 17 the Syndicate Block, located at Seventh and Rosser, went up in flames, consuming the lives of four people.

Another wartime feature of Brandon was the Alien Detention Centre created in the Winter Fair Building at Tenth and Victoria. Here during the early years of the war, hundreds of men were kept in detention. One man was shot dead trying to escape. The fears that Central European immigrants might engage in espionage or sabotage typified the emotional climate of the times.

Military training, Camp Hughes, World War I

The war years were also characterized by a growing reform movement in Manitoba which directly affected community life in Brandon. The long-sought right of women to vote in provincial elections was acquired in January, 1916. The Brandon Council of Women had campaigned for this reform. Indeed, in 1915 the Council had helped to elect Brandon's first woman to public office when Mrs. Margaret Irwin was elected to the school board. Not, however, without a note of irony: she had been nominated by two men, one of whom she succeeded in the subsequent election.

The Temperance Movement had also been active in Brandon and undoubtedly social life was dealt a sobering blow when on June 1, 1916 the provincial Temperance Act made the purchase and consumption of liquor illegal without a doctor's prescription. It is reported that a twenty-six ounce bottle of rye whisky quickly emerged as the panacea for a variety of aches, pains, and other complaints. The drought was to end in 1923.

November 11, 1918 marked the end of four years of devastation in Europe. In Brandon, victory was celebrated and the city prepared to greet the returning heroes; those who did not return were honoured in 1924 by the construction of the Cross of Sacrifice in the Brandon Cemetery.

The War's end ushered in a period of social stress in Brandon, stemming from an economic slump and the problem of finding employment for returning soldiers. The slump was signalled by the fall in the price of wheat from an average price of $3.19 a bushel in December, 1920 to $1.10 a bushel in August, 1922; the purchasing power of a bushel of wheat in 1922 was equivalent to only sixty-eight percent of that in 1912. Not until 1924 did the farmer's selling price for most agricultural produce reach profitable levels. Matters were worsened by the drought which affected southwestern Manitoba during the years 1919 to 1923.

The cast of a play enacting women's early struggle for voting privilege

Inevitably, these conditions depressed the Brandon economy and multiplied the problems of municipal finance. The economic stresses and strains were reflected by no fewer than three general strikes in Brandon during the immediate postwar period. The strikes began in the spring of 1919 with a Civic Employees' Union strike, which was followed by another in support of the Winnipeg General Strike. This period of labour strife ended in April, 1922 with the so-called Teachers' Strike, which resulted in the dismissal of the city's entire teaching staff. The growing frustration of labour with spiralling inflation, low wages, and indifferent governments was made evident in 1920 by the election of A.E. Smith, a Dominion Labour Party candidate, as Brandon's Member of the Provincial Legislature.

The Royal North West Mounted Police Detachment, C troop, at Brandon, 1919-20

Renewed prosperity and increased immigration to the West after 1924 revived the city's economy. Though municipal government was still plagued with increasing taxes to meet expenses, particularly those incurred by the street railway, the general prosperity of the times and the persistent success of Harry Cater in mayoralty elections marks the period of the late 1920's as the "era of Cater and prosperity".

With prosperity came an increasing number of automobiles on the streets of Brandon. In 1922 there were 1,400; five years later 2,804 automobiles were registered in Brandon and district. In addition, the late 1920's was an eventful period for a number of other reasons: business prospered and the rural isolation of a decade previous ended as a result of the growth of graded roads leading to Brandon; Brandon became the northern terminus for the Sunshine Highway, so called because it extended south all the way to Texas; and telephone lines now stretched into the rural areas and combined with improved mail service and increasing numbers of radios to reduce the contrast in lifestyle between town and countryside.

However, the pervasive changes in social attitudes wrought by the new technologies — transportation and communication — waited for the future. In the "Roaring Twenties", Brandonites remained "fast wedded to the old ways in manners and morals". When Martha Ostenso, a graduate of Brandon Collegiate Institute, published *Wild Geese*, a novel set in the Interlake region and which was subsequently to become a minor Canadian classic, mild scandal resulted because of the modest realism employed in the treatment of male-female relationships. Miss Ostenso's subsequent elopement to the United States with Douglas Durkin, another Manitoba writer and a married man, seemed to confirm in the eyes of some Brandonites the perversity of the arts and artists.

Prosperity had revived in the noonday sun of the 1920's, and now as the decade reached its eventide the farmers of Manitoba harvested a bumper crop; and in town and country, people were inclined, against instinct and experience, to believe without hesitation in the future and in themselves.

Dr. Powers and friends in front of Park School, ca. 1910

The spring of 1929 was not unusual; however, as summer gave way to fall the beginning of the most intense and lengthy drought to strike the Canadian West lay like a pall over the land; a thousand miles away on Wall Street stock prices dipped, then plummetted. The Great Depression had begun.

In the countryside around Brandon drought, hordes of grasshoppers in midsummer, rust, and Russian thistle slowed the germination and stunted the growth of crop after crop. It was this and the thirty-two cents a bushel for wheat in 1932 that spelled the meaning of the Depression years for farmers in southwestern Manitoba.

In Brandon local tax revenue dwindled, relief costs rose, and municipal debt became overwhelming. Brandon's finances were eventually placed under a provincially-appointed supervisor in 1936. Ironically, little help could be expected from a provincial government which in 1935 expended $5,934,402 of its $14,097,549 provincial budget simply to service debt.

In 1932 ten percent of Brandon families, i.e. 459, were receiving relief vouchers for food, fuel, and shelter; no provision was made for such necessities as toothpaste, razor blades, a newspaper, or entertainment. By 1934 some 512 families were experiencing the austerity of a relief system which had been designed to give temporary assistance to immigrant labour.

Unemployment became the lot of many; the transient workless could be seen along Pacific Avenue huddled in the "jungles" where the homeless and foot-loose lived before moving on. Many young men from Brandon waited out the Depression years doing relief work in the new Riding Mountain National Park, or working on some Depression years' boondoggle.

"Don't laugh at us today. You may be in our ranks tomorrow." Unemployed on parade, ca. 1931

The Depression years left a generation marked indelibly by privation and loss of dignity. It also transformed the politics and invalidated much of the conventional economic wisdom of the time.

In 1935, before leaving for the rigours of the British House of Lords, Prime Minister R.B. Bennett assaulted the credulity of the electorate with his new-found compassion for the victims of the Depression. To the surprise of only a few, the Royal Commission on Price Spreads allowed that corporate capitalism "harboured behind its imposing facade so much that needs cleansing". On the dusty banks of the Assiniboine Brandon lay, on the surface at least, a veritable "hotbed of quietism".

Though Harry Cater had been defeated in 1931 and T.A. Crerar, Brandon's Member of Parliament and a Liberal Cabinet Minister, had not survived the 1930 federal election, Brandonites remained moderate in their politics. It was not until 1943 that a Co-operative Commonwealth Federation candidate was elected to the Manitoba legislature from Brandon.

In Europe during the Thirties anarchy was being loosed. It was said that the "best lacked all conviction while the worst . . . (were) full of passionate intensity", and now as the decade closed, the stage was being arranged for the opening of World War II in September, 1939.

Canada's declaration of war on September 10, 1939 resulted in the enlistment of over 400 Brandon and district men in the armed forces and 100 women in the Women's Army Corps. It also created a labour shortage and by June, 1941 only two percent of the Brandon work force was without regular employment.

While the wartime labour shortage brought novel vocational opportunities for women, war also ushered in austerity. Gasoline, meat, coffee, sugar, and butter were rationed. Women's nylon stockings ceased to be.

The war also brought the dull, persistent drone of airplanes to the skies over Brandon after the city was named an air force training centre for pilots from around the Commonwealth.

Airmen from Commonwealth Air Training Plan, guests in a Brandon home, 1942

Brandon families, of course, were not spared the tragedy of war. Brandon men were among the Grenadiers who left Jamaica on their fateful trip to Hong Kong and prisoner of war status. Doubtless there were sons of the Wheat City present when the Second Canadian Division landed on the murderous beaches of Dieppe in the spring of 1942. By the end of the war, no fewer than sixty-eight graduates of Brandon Collegiate had died in the service of their country.

The period of readjustment following the war was surprisingly free of the problems that had plagued the city after World War I. There were the inevitable problems of inflation and increasing wage demands after wartime price and wage controls were lifted. But, after years of depression and war, apprehension soon gave way to optimism about the future. This was reflected in the sharply increasing birthrate which soon turned into a veritable baby boom.

To meet the housing needs of an expanding population, the city spread south and west. New educational and recreational facilities were constructed. Brandon's economic base continued to grow throughout the period and the range of services and shopping facilities increased as Eighteenth Street and Victoria Avenue developed as competitors to Rosser Avenue as commercial arteries.

In 1975 Brandon's population had grown to 35,500. The average age was somewhat older than that of Brandon's population in the years immediately after the war; families were smaller. However, here was a population more affluent, more mobile, and better educated than any in the history of the city. Gone were the days of 1947 when homes on the north side of the CPR tracks were not served by the City's sewage system and when, of the 4,015 dwellings in Brandon, only 32 percent had mechanical refrigerators, 53 percent had phones, and 32 percent had automobiles. Still, progress is a double-edged sword and, while growing material affluence has enriched the lives of Brandonites, nostalgia for the bygone Brandon of horses, iceboxes, corner stores, and close neighbourhoods persists among the old and the not-so-old.

As the city approaches its centenary, there is much to celebrate and little that does not bear recall of the days since that "happy army of young men" arrived to claim a share of the opportunities awaiting them in the Wonder City of the Northwest.

T.S. Mitchell

# Mayors of the City of Brandon

Twenty-seven men have served as mayors of Brandon since the city was incorporated in 1882. Photographs are not available of W. Winter, mayor in 1883, and Charles Adams, 1887.

Thomas Mayne Daly
1882; 1884

James A. Smart
1885 - 1886; 1895 - 1896

Alexander C. Fraser
1888 - 1899; 1901 - 1902

Andrew Kelly
1890 - 1891

Dr. John McDiarmid
1892 - 1894; 1899 - 1900

Ezekial Evans
1897 - 1898

Robert Hall
1903 - 1904

John W. Fleming
1905; 1906 - 1911; 1912; 1913

Stephen E. Clement
1907 - 1908

Henry L. Adolph
1909 - 1910

J. H. Hughes
1914

H. W. Cater
1915 - 1918; 1922 - 1931, 1934 - 1937

A. R. McDiarmid
1919

George Dinsdale
1920 - 1921

E. Fotheringham
1932 - 1933

F. H. Young
1938 - 1943

L. H. McDorman
1944 - 1945

Frank T. Williamson
1946 - 1951

James Creighton
1952 - 1955; 1958 - 1961

Dr. Stuart Schultz
1956 - 1957

Stephen A. Magnacca
1962 - 1969

W. K. Wilton
1970 - 1974

Elwood C. Gorrie
1975 - 1977

G. D. Box
1978

28

Photograph by H.R. Hugh Davis
Freelance Photographer

**His Worship Ken Burgess**
**Mayor of Brandon**
**1979 - 1980**
**1981 -**

# Message from the Mayor

Brandon's Centennial — 1982 — is a very special event and the preparation of its celebration has joined people together in a common cause, working side by side to fill the year with twelve months of happy occasions. This Centennial publication of the history of Brandon is one of many projects, and will serve not only as a keepsake to remind us of our roots and traditions, but will mark the beginning of a new era.
To our Centennial Chairman, Eva Campbell, her committee and all organizations and individuals involved, a sincere "thank you". A warm welcome is extended to all visitors to our city, with a very special welcome to all former residents who will return home during 1982.
As we enjoy the celebration of our 100th anniversary, we must remember with pride the foresight, ingenuity and determination of our forefathers. They had a vision, and we and all future generations must have the motivation, determination and character to add to the foundation that has been created for us in this community.
The past is the basis upon which to build for the future, and as Norman Vincent Peale once wrote, "Salute your future with hope and faith, trust God and go ahead with anticipation." Let's all join together in celebrating this special occasion. Happy 100th birthday, Brandon!

# The "Brandon" Story

This cairn commemorates the arrival of the first pioneers to settle in the Brandon Hills, in the 1880's. It is from the Brandon Hills that our city received its name. The first Brandon House was established by Donald McKay for the Hudson's Bay Company in 1793. "Mad" Donald, as he was known, had been located at the Hudson's Bay trading post at the mouth of the Albany River where it flows into James Bay, from which he was sent by the

Company to establish a trading post on the Assiniboine.

The Hudson's Bay Company had also established a supply post on Charlton Island in a cove sheltered by a "bare hill of sand" called Brandon Hill. (This post remained functional until 1932.) In a book which records the early voyage of Captain James of Bristol, written in 1633, the Captain reported a dreadful winter spent on Charlton Island, in the Bay which bears his name, where they had to bury their chief mate. This they did "on the top of a bare hill of sand, which we cald *Brandon Hill*." A footnote in the book explains that the name derived from Brandon Hill, which forms a portion of the seaport city of Bristol, England.

Brandon Hill in Bristol was once a fortification. It dominates the seaport from which sailed a British trader, John Cabot, and his sons in 1496 on a voyage of discovery for King Henry VII of England. This photo shows the tower that was erected on Brandon Hill in memory of John Cabot. How Brandon Hill in Bristol got its name is a fascinating story, one which historian Roy Brown will be telling in his forthcoming book, *The Brandon Hill Connection.*
    Whether or not "Mad" Donald McKay ever saw Brandon

Hill, Bristol, is not known; certainly he knew of Brandon Hill on Charlton Island in James Bay. We can reasonably assume that when he arrived at the confluence of the Assiniboine and the Souris to establish the trading post he noted the escarpment that rose to the northwest. It resembled the one which had been familiar to him in James Bay, so he named it *Brandon Hill* and the trading post *Brandon House.*

# I Brandon — a certainty, not a prospect

When the flood tide of immigration struck the Canadian West, it was inevitable that a second city should rise west of the Provincial capital. Brandon's location had the advantage of being far enough from Winnipeg that its growth would not be threatened by proximity to that city; yet it served, as it still does, as a commercial centre for the western part of the province. The prospects for Brandon's growth were such that some prophesied that it would even exceed that of Winnipeg. History has not confirmed this expectation, but it has proved the necessity for an urban centre between the capital cities of Manitoba and Saskatchewan. Brandon is filling that role.

Here is the Dougald McVicar family, from L to R: Gilman, Lily, Hugh, Mrs. McVicar, Dougald McVicar, Hattie, Will; seated front: Wesley, Jasper (on Dougald's lap), Effie.

"In June of 1878, my father [Dougald McVicar], along with his brother, Uncle John McVicar, started for Manitoba, leaving their families in the East until they were located. They reached St. Boniface by train and then crossed over the Red River by ferry to Winnipeg. From there they started out on foot with their necessities on their backs and walked up around Gladstone and Minnedosa and other places until finally they stopped by the banks of the Assiniboine River about 130 miles west of Winnipeg, being better satisfied with the location, soil, etc., here than in any other place they had seen . . . . This place was afterward named Grand Valley by my mother, who arrived in Winnipeg September 12, 1879."

— Lily McVicar
*Brandon — some early day history — beginning with Grand Valley.*

"Father built a large ferry boat run by a cable across the river and an open boat and paddles.

"During the winter of 1879, my father had a gang of men in the bush near Sewell cutting logs and, early in the spring of 1880, he had them drawn to Grand Valley in sleighs. During that summer, he built a large log warehouse as a landing place for the steamers. Mr. Clement (who was afterward Sheriff Clement of Brandon), and one of his boys, coming through on the steamer with a lot of household luggage which in some way had got soaking wet, were among the first to welcome this big log warehouse where everything could be spread out to dry and left there, returning for same later in the evening."

— Lily McVicar

An Indian camp such as this one was a familiar sight to the first settlers. Although they and the Indians first regarded one another with suspicion, they found they could usually establish a mutual trust. An early pioneer, Mrs. Eliza Durston, writing about coming west in 1882, said: "I was never frightened of the Indians. I used to invite them into the house and serve them tea and something to eat and they used to like getting tobacco." Many settlers, in turn, obtained pemmican from the Indians to supplement their own food supplies.

These Red River carts are bringing settlers with their basic effects to the North West Territories — some, perhaps, to the new settlement at Grand Valley. Dougald McVicar said of these early carts that the sound they made "was very musical but lacked harmony."

A survey party has set up its camp in the Brandon area, June, 1882. William Van Horne was in charge of the party sent out by the CPR to do the survey. Peter Merrick was hired for ten dollars a day as chief surveyor. The original survey stick was planted near the present-day corner of First and Pacific. Whether the streets should be 99 feet wide or 66 feet was a contentious decision. The prospect of financial advantage to the Railway influenced the choice of the narrower width. Colonel Rosser himself had a vested interest in land in this new location of the infant city. So, one hundred years later, we have numerous one-way streets in the main business section.

The *SS Marquette* is shown here taking on cordwood and lumber at this landing on the Red River.

Built in Moorhead, North Dakota for a pioneer entrepreneur, Peter McArthur, the *Marquette* was considered the most popular of the several riverboats that plied the Assiniboine between 1879 and 1882. She had a cargo capability of 170 tons and cabin accommodation for fifty passengers, but could carry as many as 350.

In May of 1879, Captain Jerry Webber brought her up the Assiniboine on her first trip from Winnipeg to the Hudson's Bay Company post at Fort Ellice, located some two miles from where the village of St. Lazare now stands. She took nine days to go upriver but returned in five.

In May of 1881, she carried to Grand Valley some of the first of the flood of settlers to establish homes in the Northwest. In a statement of appreciation of the fine trip enjoyed by some twenty-eight people who came to Grand Valley, they expressed their expectations that a town will grow that "is likely indeed to become one of the great cities on the continent."

The *Marquette* made her last trip on the Assiniboine in 1882, after which she served on the Red between Winnipeg and the region around Selkirk until 1888.

The County of Brandon, established in 1881, was comprised of a group of five municipalities including townships 7 to 12 in ranges 16 to 22 West inclusive. In 1883 the City of Brandon was added to the County. Back row: Reeve Pettit, Daly; Reeve Clegg, Elton; Reeve Charles Whitehead, Cornwallis. Front row: Reeve Steele, Glenwood; W. A. Macdonald, county solicitor; Reeve Hannah, Whitehead; J. Weatherall, county clerk; J. H. Brownlee, county engineer.

Almost a quarter of a century of leadership to the City of Brandon has been given by these former mayors. Their terms were consecutively served from 1938 to 1961. This photo was taken at the time of Brandon's 75th birthday celebrations in 1957 when Dr. Stuart Schultz, centre, was Mayor. The others, from L. to R. are Fred Young, L. H. McDorman, Frank Williamson, and James Creighton.

This trim little locomotive, built for the Northern Pacific Railway in 1872, was bought by Joseph Whitehead and transported to Winnipeg in 1877. In 1883 the Canadian Pacific bought her for $5,800 and put her to work following the construction of the Railway across the prairies. Better known as the Countess of Dufferin, she spent some years at Canmore, Alberta at the mines, and at Golden, B.C. hauling lumber before coming back to her final resting place in Winnipeg. The people of Golden still feel that Old Betsy, as they called her out there, is living under false pretences in Winnipeg. Her spirit is in the mountains, they say.

## FREE PRESS EXTRA.

### MONDAY, OCT. 8, 1877.

#### The First Locomotive in the North-West!

#### To Arrive this Afternoon!

#### Celebration of the Event!

Intelligence has just been received that the first locomotive and tender, with a caboose and six flat cars, which are being brought down for the Pembina Branch by Mr. Joseph Whitehead, will arrive here this afternoon at about four o'clock by the steamer Selkirk.

Notwithstanding the short notice, we understand that a fitting reception will be tendered; and the mayor and corporation, it is understood, will take the necessary steps for the proper recognition of this important event in the history of the North-West.

The steamer will probably stop at No. 6 warehouse, foot of Post-office street.

Let there be a grand rally of citizens on the occasion!

Undoubtedly the Countess deserved this Extra issue of the *Free Press* to announce her arrival in the West in 1877.

In May of 1881, Joseph Whitehead's son, Charles, established the first lumber business in Brandon, but retired the following year to carry on a large farming operation immediately south of the city. The Whitehead family has owned the controlling interest in the *Brandon Sun* since 1903.

Beecham Trotter in his book, *Horseman in the West*, relates that Coombs and Stewart had set up a temporary business in Grand Valley on what was a lane until such time as they could purchase a lot. Then, learning that the land across the river was being considered for the founding of the railway town, they simply "took down their store in sections, carried it to the boat and shipped it and their stock of goods to the same landing place as had received Whitehead's barge load of lumber. They set it up again on the corner of Sixth and Pacific Avenue on the same day."

Here they are, Brandon's first merchants, equipped to sell the settlers' first provisions. Mr. Stewart is the gentleman in shirtsleeves.

Starting as a clerk with Coombs and Stewart was Wm. Muir, who came to Brandon from Ontario in October, 1881. Working from 8 a.m. to 10 p.m. and sometimes till midnight, he received $15 a month. In 1888 he started this grocery business at 140 Sixth Street, and here he stayed for 56 years.

Here is the best business location in Brandon in 1882 — the corner of Sixth and Rosser, looking towards Pacific Avenue.

"One of the greatest boons ever conferred upon the tavelling public of the North-west was the opening of this fine hotel in April of the present year (1882)." The description goes on to say that the hotel can accommodate 100 guests, the upper floor being exclusively dormitories. "Both [proprietors Messrs. Carson and Caulfield] have other branches of business on hand, but in none have they furnished a more useful institution, and one that will do more for the progress of Brandon than the Grand Central Hotel."

Jas. A. Smart's business here is a $15,000 stock of hardware, paints, glass, and such. Mr. Smart was elected one of Brandon's first aldermen — having shown himself "one of her most enterprising and public-spirited citizens". He later served two terms as mayor of the city, and represented Brandon in the Provincial Legislature. He was appointed deputy to the Minister of the Interior, Clifford Sifton.

The year is 1905. Imagine yourself standing in the middle of Rosser Avenue at the Eleventh Street intersection, looking east. The space at the extreme left will eventually accommodate the Bank of Montreal (our present Library). A couple of rigs stand in front of the Post Office, and the building on this side of it is the Union Bank of Canada. The top floor of the Fraser Block, 1027 Rosser Avenue, was one of the earlier locations of Professor McKee's Academy when it was moved here from Rapid City in 1890. It became known as Brandon College in 1897.

Obviously, this is not a one-way street, for whatever way is most convenient is the way to go. Paving is in the future.

Rosser Avenue appears a bit untidy here at the corner of Eighth, as the photographer looks west this day in 1896.

Beyond the first telephone pole at the left is the location of the Nation and Shewan store — 816 Rosser — just about where the Metropolitan store stands today, surrounded by the Brandon Gallery.

In the distance you can barely see the sign that is still quite legible almost a hundred years later. That is where The Soup Kettle simmers today at 1031 Rosser Avenue.

Could Brandon's first library have been located here, behind those two windows above the sacks? The signs say READING ROOM.

The Brunswick Hotel was located on the west side of Tenth Street at Pacific Avenue. There must have been some good reason for having the reading room almost next door to the BAR ROOM.

Looking west from Sixth Street, we see a busy Rosser Avenue, with prospects of a confrontation between two teams of horses. Yaeger's Furs had not yet been established in this building at the immediate left. The date of this photo is given as 1886 — our city is four years old.

Some ninety years after the *Marquette* made her last trip on the Assiniboine, her spirit returned to help Grand Valley Council plan for the celebration of Manitoba's Centennial in 1970.

Established in 1969 by the Brandon Chamber of Commerce, this Council includes, from L. to R.: Alex Jackson, George Murray, Mayor Steve Magnacca, Roy Brown (co-ordinator of events for Grand Valley Days), Vince Dodds, and Garth Stouffer. This Council initiated the establishment of the Assiniboine Historical Society in 1970, with Garth Stouffer its first president.

These replicas of the *Marquette* and the carts were given to VIP's visiting the City during those celebrations.

# II Wonder City of the Northwest

As early as 1887 an unknown author wrote "A Condensed History of Brandon" in which he described the city's growth in this way: "Among the very wonderful creations which have sprung out of the railway development of the Northwest during the past five years, none is more striking than the growth and substantial progress made by the City of Brandon." A similar "striking growth" has been effected in later periods of the City's history, prompted by or resulting from some outstanding event: street paving and the building of the street railway system prior to the Dominion Fair in July, 1913; the post-war housing boom paralleled by construction of educational and care institutions; the development of shopping centres and business and protection agencies; the mushrooming of new motels and restaurants prior to the Canada Winter Games in 1979. Photographs depicting some of this expansion are included in the following pages.

This photo of McVicar's brickyard first appeared in *The Dominion Illustrated*, August 31, 1889. The brickyard, according to one historic record, was located near Carberry. Lily McVicar writes: " . . . when Father started the brickyard in the Valley, Mr. Earl was his foreman and took charge of the making of the brick". One might infer, however, from the following, that a second brickyard had been established: " . . . I never remember going to and from our South Brickyard home without passing by and admiring the Old Crystal Palace, with its pretty colored glass and odd shape." (The Crystal Palace was at the Exhibition Grounds.)

According to an early description of Brandon's first businesses, this view shows Ninth Street between Pacific and Rosser Avenues looking to the northeast. The firm of Wesbrook and Fairchild Agricultural Implements and the building at the south corner are in the location later developed by John A. MacDonald for a men's clothing store, presently occupied by Super Thrifty Drug Store.

The large white building with the fencing is the Western Hotel. Barely discernible in the background is the old Rapid City Trail.

This view across the street shows a covered wagon that has just pulled up in front of the Canadian Pacific Express office on Rosser Avenue. Immigrants from the United States usually arrived with this type of vehicle. The little shop called The New Era, next door to Fortier and Bucke, was described in 1882 as "quite a novelty in Brandon . . . simply a cozy little room on Rosser Avenue where the most fastidious patron of the weed may select a cigar, pipe, or packet of tobacco to suit his taste, or the liquid connoisseur may indulge in a temperance drink".

This architect's design of the prospective Hughes Block was prepared by W. H. Shillinglaw, who arrived in Brandon March 1, 1882. The plan shows the potential for future growth of the building that was erected only up to the second level. It stands today at the corner of Tenth Street and Princess Avenue, as it was in 1904. Hughes and Company offices are still located in this block.

We believe this photo deserves being located in this section — The Wonder City of the Northwest. Note the dates of construction and search in vain for comparable records in more recent construction projects.

The Roman Catholic denomination was comprised of over 200 persons in 1882, and arrangements were made to allocate $6,000 for the construction of a church. The south-west corner of Third Street and Lorne Avenue was purchased in April, 1883 by Archbishop Taché of St. Boniface as a site for St. Joseph's Convent. The building was completed in May of the same year in order to "bribe" the Sisters of the Faithful Companions of Jesus to establish a school in Brandon. Five Sisters arrived in the summer of 1883, took up residence in the Convent, and began classes for fifteen children on October 8 of that year. By 1890 there were ninety pupils attending, but by 1895 the enrollment had declined to thirty.

The Sisters left Brandon that year, and the school was closed.

In 1899 four Sisters of Our Lady of the Missions arrived in Brandon, took possession of the Convent, and re-opened the school on September 1 with fifty pupils.

Mayor Fleming drives the first
spike for the Brandon Street
Railway, October 9, 1911, on
Tenth Street near Rosser Avenue.
"We are here to witness a start on
one of the most important things
that make for progress and
development," he said.

Tearing up streets is an essential part of Brandon's development. Brandon ratepayers had approved, in June, 1910, the cost of $140,000 to build the railway; however, the matter of ownership and operation had not been decided. Another referendum November 9, 1911 gave approval to inviting private ownership bids. A British syndicate, represented by Brandon resident, J. D. McGregor, was chosen April 10, 1912 to complete the line started by the City, and to operate it for thirty years.

Despite the passing of the referendum, however, there was sufficient objection voiced against the terms of the agreement to induce Mr. McGregor to withdraw his claim. Another plebiscite held June 14, 1912 once again gave approval to public ownership, and also to a $300,000 construction by-law.

Mr. Speakman, the City Engineer, again got operations under way. Mr. David Heatley, on loan from the CPR, was master tracklayer, and William Wakefield acted as timekeeper for the working crew of recently-arrived immigrants from Poland and Galicia. The overhead work was done largely by men from the United States.

Powered by electricity obtained from the Brandon Electric Light Company, the trial run of the first street cars took place May 16, 1913, and regular service began June 2, 1913.

With flags flying, Brandon street car service gets under way in June, 1913. One route went along Tenth Street, turning west to Thirteenth Street then south to the Exhibition Grounds. Another went east to Percy Street, and the western service extended as far as 24th Street.

Traffic appears somewhat disorganized on this occasion. The newly-established street car service is being impeded by the horse-drawn vehicles and the people in front of the Winter Fair Building on Tenth Street.

It was at this very corner, Tenth and McTavish, that an accident occurred the day after the street railway service was inaugurated. A nervous motorist stalled her vehicle right in the face of an oncoming street car. Before she could get mobile, the transit car struck and sent her flying.

Recently-appointed Police Chief Berry took a hard line with traffic offenders, particularly with one of the city aldermen who questioned the Chief's authority in charging him with a traffic violation at Tenth and Rosser. The Chief fined him two dollars.

One old-timer recalls that Saturday nights were busy in Brandon during these First World War years. You couldn't drive a vehicle on Rosser Avenue for the crowds. Stores stayed open till late, and a festive air prevailed.

Street car operations did not inferfere with important functions along the regular route.

Could this have been one of our earlier Travellers' Day Parades? This route along Tenth Street is still taken for parades today. Only the cars are different — they bear 1924 license plates. And they have an unusual (to us in 1981) parking pattern on the west side.

Doig's still does business where the Doig, Rankin & Robertson, Limited firm was located.

Many of the operational crew were former motormen and conductors from Great Britain. Reporting for duty for the first car in the morning, or returning home after the last car at night, in the dead of winter was a bitter experience for some of the British immigrants. Some of the men can be identified, counting from left to right.

Bottom row: 1. Charles Dinsdale 3. J. Gordon 4. W. Green 5. Harry Cater 7. Thomas Boden 8. Wm. Young 9. Frank Henry

Centre row: 1. J. Roy 3. A. Gordon 9. Ted Jones 12. F. W. Spedding 14. Archie Ferguson

Top row: 1. Tony Scott 2. Herbert Smith 4. George Chidley 5. Archie Goucher 6. Jack Watkins

Brandon's street railway proved to be too great a financial burden for the city during the early Thirties. In 1932 work started on ripping up the tracks. The service had lasted only twenty years. A jitney service was then put into use and Brandon citizens had second thoughts about their decision to have street car service discontinued.

MacArthur and Sons instituted the first bus service in July, 1932. Brandon taxpayers continued for another twenty years to pay for a street railway system that no longer existed.

Here is MacArthur's first bus approaching a block or so away.

Some of the rolling stock of Brandon's street railway was put to good use in the tourist park. Other cars were placed on the south side of Victoria Avenue near 25th Street to be used as coffee bars and an ice cream stand, but they have long since disappeared as the residential area pushed westward.

47

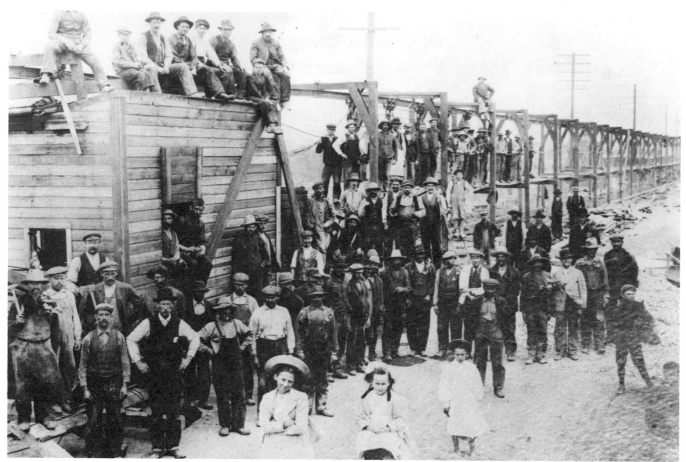

As the street paving and railway construction program was progressing, so also did the sewer construction. This photo shows the crew that built the sewer line along Pacific Avenue from Fifth Street to the outlet under the First Street bridge.

Immigrants from Europe form the greater portion of this crew. The building shown dimly at the end of this earth conveyance structure was one of Brandon's three breweries, the Empire Brewery.

The Canadian Northern Railway's $500,000 investment in the building of this luxury hotel in Brandon in 1911 proves they regarded it as the "Wonder City of the Northwest".

Beset by such problems as material shortages, accidents, and strikes, the Prince Edward finally opened June 19, 1912. The opening event was a charity ball to aid an extension to the General Hospital.

The "Prince Eddy" was built largely of local brick, faced with brick imported from Belgium. The furnishings originally ordered for the hotel went down with the *Titanic* in April, 1912.

In 1919 the Hotel invited clients to come in for "tea and a chat with friends" every afternoon from four to six o'clock — "when you've got the blues" — for 25 cents.

It took two years to build the "Eddy". On February 24, 1980, it took less than two minutes to level, by implosion, this wing. Today, the property is a parking lot, awaiting the Midas touch of some developer.

Inside the City Market, in the Arena on Tenth Street, here is a typical crowd on a good day in late fall, 1911.

PROVINCIAL FRUIT SHOW, BRANDON, 1935.

The entire floor space of the Arena (part of the same City Market complex) has been used for this Provincial Fruit Show in 1935.

THE MIDWAY, ANNUAL EXHIBITION, BRANDON MAN.

The first wild animal show came to Brandon in 1909. We get a hint of the excitement of the big top shows located here behind the grandstand.

It is 1913, the year of the Dominion Fair which used to be held annually in some major Canadian city. This is Brandon's year! Here are but a few of the 200,000 people that are said to have visited the City during the ten days of the Fair. This building, the Crystal Palace, was demolished in the 1930's.

The midway at Brandon Fair in the 1920's led ultimately to the grandstand. People are still nostalgic about this grandstand which, in the name of progress, came down in the late Sixties.

Some thirty years later, the crowds seem to have thinned out. Here is an interesting study of the fashions of the day. Drapes are in; women's skirts are shorter, but not much!

A volunteer fire brigade of some twenty men was organized in November, 1882. Here are some members of that first organization.

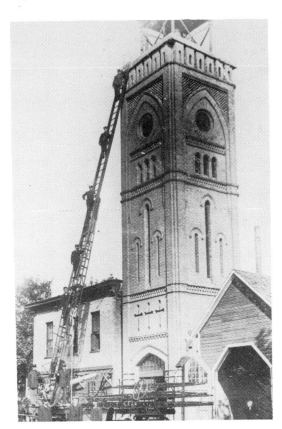

This photo, taken in 1905, shows the horse-drawn equipment. In the early days of the Department's service, horses were not housed at the station and, at the alarm, the first horses to arrive were harnessed for action.

The Brandon Firemen's Ball is a tradition that has, except for the last few years, been maintained throughout the Department's history. Reading an account of the firemen's ball that opened the new City Hall and Opera House on February 29, 1892, we realize that fire prevention standards have come a long way; for example, "... the hall had been handsomely and carefully decorated; evergreens hanging in graceful festoons; banners, bannerettes and bunting (red, white and blue) gave a richness and added an effect that was heightened by the brightness of electric lamps, placed in profusion in all parts of the spacious building".

*Firemen's Annual Ball*

*The Officers and Members of Brandon Fire Dept. and the Firemen's Benevolent Society request the pleasure of the company of*

Mr. _____ *and Ladies*

*at their 20th Annual Ball given in the Opera House on Monday Evening, January 2nd, 1911, at 8 o'clock*

*First-class Orchestra will furnish music.*
Committee—Capt. R. S. Daley, G. Taylor, A. Partridge
Admission—Gentlemen, $2.00

J. Melhuish, Chief                              A. Elborne, Sec'y

*From Mrs Ardiel A.C*

In 1884 when this Brandon Courthouse was completed, it was one of the City's most imposing buildings. In 1910 it was remodelled to become the Provincial Gaol and served as such until 1980 when the occupants were moved to a new building called The Brandon Correctional Institution. The old courthouse building, with its formerly well-maintained gardens, now awaits development as some other institution.

Classic in its design, this Court House was built in 1908 in the more convenient location at Princess and Eleventh.

Henry Barlow, a stern administrator of the law in Brandon for some thirty years, joined the Police force in 1915. From 1926 until his retirement in 1945, he was Detective-sergeant of the force. It has been said of him that he was "a very thorough officer — he lived his job". His life was threatened during a night chase in 1919, when he was wounded by a bullet from the fugitives.

54

W. A. Elliott, one of Brandon's early architects, designed the YMCA building that is shown under construction on Eighth Street. The cornerstone laying ceremony, 1905, is taking place.

Brandon claims the distinction of being the first city in the Canadian Northwest to be lighted by electricity. On February 19, 1889 the first lights were turned on, generated from a direct current system. In 1892 an alternating system was established. Early in the century, this dam on the Little Saskatchewan River supplied the power for electricity. The dam was also a popular fishing spot.

This photo, circa 1965, shows many of Brandon's important early buildings still standing.

# III   The City of Opportunity

Yesterday's dream, tomorrow's future? What dreams of the future inspired Brandon's first pioneers to come west? Some had plans of making the fast dollar and returning east; others held a vision of creating a rich new life in this raw land. Opportunities not available to them in older provinces awaited them here — opportunities to be caught by exercising brawn or wit, or both. After experiencing the flood of 1882 and the subsequent sudden blizzard in May that destroyed countless tents, many decided that Brandon, Manitoba was not their cup o'tea. The first train to leave Brandon after these disasters pulled three coaches filled with disillusioned men and women. But the enduring story of Brandon is, of course, to be told in the achievements of those who stayed.

No, this is not an old English inn; it's the CPR station on Pacific Avenue, built in 1887.

Less rural in appearance is this scene at the front of the CPR station in 1906. Meeting the trains was once a popular summertime diversion, just to see who were coming and going.

The Railway provided many opportunities for steady employment for British and Central European immigrants.

The "section house", built for the railway section foreman, was one of the first permanent homes to be constructed in towns and villages as the railway lines crossed the prairies. Two such buildings (always painted red with white) are shown centre and right in this very early photo of Brandon.

This Silk Train is having a brief pause at one of the few scheduled stops in its race across Canada to Prescott, Ontario. There it will be ferried across the St. Lawrence to Ogdensburg, New York and continue to New York City.

"The Silk" used to make a five-minute stop in Brandon on its runs during two decades of service early in the century. During this stop the locomotive would be changed and a quick check made of the running gear.

Nothing interrupted The Silk's schedule. Even a special train bearing Prince George (later King George VI) eastward in December, 1924 had to be pulled onto a side track to allow The Silk to pass.

Speed was essential because the railways paid a high daily insurance while the cargo was being transported. Even during the Twenties a cargo of silk leaving Yokohama on the *Empress of Canada* arrived in New York City thirteen days later. A record trip was made between Brandon and Winnipeg in 1924 — 133 miles in 131 minutes.

The Silk service was discontinued in the mid-Thirties when there was no longer a demand for silk. A former Silk fireman, Alex Stelmack, still resides in Brandon.

The diesel horn announced the arrival of a new era in railroading.

With the passing of the steam locomotive went the romance of the opening of the West. People of the present generation have no nostalgic recollection of the wail of the train in the dead of night. To the homesteader it was comforting to know that other human beings were on their way to help relieve the loneliness of prairie life.

The first diesel came to Brandon on January 12, 1950.

This Immigration Hall, first constructed in 1904 on Pacific at Twelfth, served in several capacities besides that of a temporary home for early immigrants. During the 1918 flu epidemic, it was used as an infirmary. In the Thirties it was a hostel for hundreds of unemployed who travelled across the country seeking jobs. It finally served as a storage shed for farm implements.

When it was moved to Fifth and Pacific in 1906, the foundation stones were numbered to be used again as the foundation in the new location.

The Donaldson family's meat packing industry had its beginnings as far back as 1890 when Joseph Donaldson bought a butchering business on Rosser Avenue. In 1936 Brandon Packers was formed and remained a family business until the late Fifties. Today Burns Meats Limited gives employment to some 130 Brandon residents.

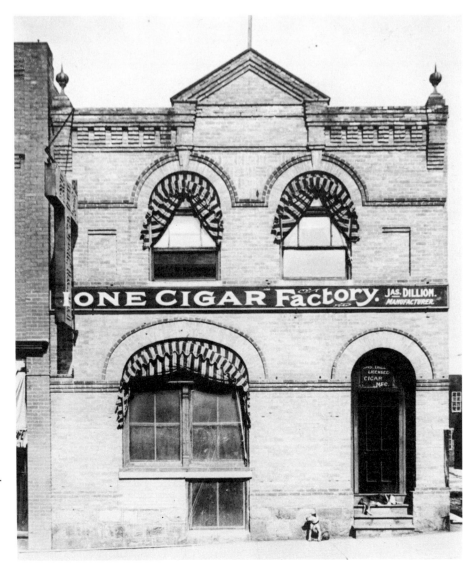

The Ione Cigar Factory, next door to the Rex Cafe in the 100 block on Tenth Street, was operating in the 1890's. A second such factory was in operation by 1903 on Pacific Avenue.

The Hanbury Manufacturing Company on Pacific Avenue turned out cabinets for stores as well as many other kinds of furniture and millwork for Brandon's first building projects. The Company moved its business to British Columbia in 1914 where lumber was more readily available.

In the spring of 1910 five million board feet of logs were brought down the Assiniboine to these mills. Some 125 lumbermen also descended on Brandon with the money earned during eight months of life in the bush, and the invasion added to the business in the bars and other less public establishments.

The original building shown in the centre of the photograph is now occupied by the Metev Woollen Mill.

This is the firm of Vivian, Riley and Garside (also known as "The Gang") at their first location on Eighth Street in August, 1882. Their business is painting and frescoing. "The faith they hold in the future of this town is sufficient to induce them to locate permanently." By September The Gang had done "a large amount of this kind of work in Brandon", and they just started business July 15, 1882!

Brandon's first restaurant was located on Pacific Avenue, a plank laid across two barrels. One could almost lay a bet that it was these two chaps who established that first eatery and have since upgraded the accommodations to include the boarding house. Anyway, they have an ideal location just opposite the CPR station. The laundry facilities appear to be adequate, providing the weather co-operates.

When Dr. Alexander Fleming first came to Brandon in May, 1881, he attended the sick and disabled from a tent. Here we see, one year later, his third place of business established at the corner of Eighth and Rosser. His volume of business increased so rapidly during the summer of 1882 that he gave up his medical practice to manage his Apothecaries' Hall.

When Dr. Fleming died in November, 1898, so great was the city's sense of loss that, for five days, hundreds of people passed by his body before the final burial.

Sophisticated display technique is still in the future for this business. Still, the goods are accessible, rain or shine, and so is the service.

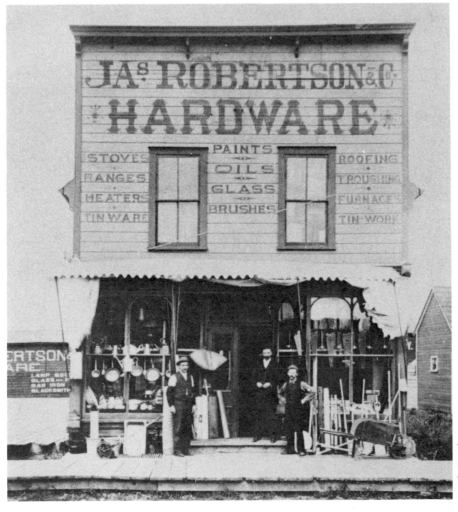

The members of this firm stand ready to provide their customers with anything from a frying pan to a wheelbarrow and lawnmower.

Wright & Wright, established in this "commodious building on Rosser Avenue", is described in 1882 as "one of the leading houses of Brandon". The business done, even before the end of their first year in Brandon, is said to have been about $25,000. Here is the entire staff.

This flourishing dry goods business, located between Thirteenth and Fourteenth Streets on Rosser Avenue, was bought out in 1906 by George Doig and John Robertson.

Mutter Brothers' Store had changed little from 1905 until they closed their door at 928 Rosser Avenue in 1975. Mutters shipped their carefully aged cheeses to customers in all parts of Canada and even to the United States. George Mutter stands behind the counter ready for business. A modified replica of this store is extant in the Daly House Museum.

Roast beef for Brandon households is on the way. Joseph Birtles, Family Butcher, was established in business before 1907 at 608 Rosser Avenue. His son, John, at the extreme right, set up his own meat business in Alexander after World War I, and continued there until 1952.

The high class dining room on the second floor of Aagaard's Restaurant on Eighth Street was a popular meeting place in the 1920's. Important banquets were held here; ladies dropped in for afternoon tea. Brandon Retail Merchants' Association held its organizational meeting here. "A number of live business men from Winnipeg and other points will be present and will speak," announced the *Brandon Sun*.

65

The George Knowlton family arrived in Brandon by train in 1882 and took up temporary residence in a large tent until their frame house was finished that fall. The house still stands on Thirteenth Street. Bruce Knowlton, one of ten children, is shown here with his bride, Edna Laidlaw. He started in business with Zink's Shoe Store, which he bought out in 1918, and established Knowlton's Boot Shop Ltd.

Rare today is the kind of craftsman shown in this photograph. John Macson, shoemaker, had his shop on Tenth Street in the 1950's. He is shown here with his young apprentice, Jake Hildebrand.

While many businesses went under during the Thirties, this enterprising woman decided to open a new business in 1934. Mona Weir's exclusive boutique on Ninth Street catered to women who were in a position to choose elegance as well as quality, with cost not being an inhibiting factor. One did not choose from the rack at Mona's; one was shown what Mona thought would be an appropriate gown or suit or accessory. The business thrived until the owner's retirement in 1975.

William Fleming peddled drinking water from this cart at five cents a pail. His well, located about Thirteenth Street near Princess, also provided water to ice a toboggan slide down the slope to Rosser. In vain, Fleming tried padlocking the pump, but somehow the locks came undone and the young scamps continued to have slick slides to the end of the block.

This 1898 photo of the south side of the 800 block on Rosser shows, among other establishments, the Nation and Shewan store. Soon after this firm started business in 1894, they donated ten percent of a week's sales to the building of Brandon's first hospital. During the 1917 harvest season when there was a scarcity of farm workers, the store's employees, along with those of some other businesses, went to work in the harvest fields in the evenings, and gave their earnings to a local patriotic fund.

In 1923 when the city library was ejected from its location on the top floor of the City Hall and seemed about to die, Nation and Shewan opened a small library from which they loaned books for two cents a week.

The Syndicate Block, built in 1892, dominated Rosser Avenue's south side between Seventh and Eighth Streets. Doig, Rankin, and Robertson were once located here until the devastating fire of 1916 drove them to find a new location on Tenth Street.

Here is a man who made the opportunity to become the kids' best friend, ca. 1925. William Chrest, who came to Brandon in 1905, was owner of Chrest's Shoe Store, but on summer evenings he drove this vehicle wherever a sports event was in progress, or wherever neighborhood kids gathered to play.

Some of the most controversial issues in Brandon's history have been related to public institutions and the buildings that house them. Here is one such building, a fine substantial structure, yet inadequate now to house the library of the ever-growing city.

It was built in 1906 as the second Merchants' Bank. Brandon's first construction strike occurred while the bank was being built. (Stonecutters were not getting their paycheques regularly and for that reason struck.)

When the Merchants' Bank failed in 1922, the Bank of Montreal acquired its assets, including this building. In 1944, after sixty years of being moved here and there into nooks and corners of various buildings, the Brandon library was again looking for a new home. The Bank of Montreal offered the City this building, and after some legislative measures were duly taken, the library was moved into the then-spacious new quarters which were to be its home for almost forty years.

This picture, taken October, 1936 in front of Clark Hall, shows, from the left, Brandon College's first principal, Dr. A. P. McDiarmid; President J. R. C. Evans; and Dr. H. L. MacNeill, Dean of Arts 1921 - 1926 and Acting President 1926 - 1928.

Brandon College campus has undergone remarkable changes in the last two decades of its more than eighty years' history. In 1960 only the original buildings shown in the foreground, and constructed in 1901, dominated the campus. Some thirty years before, the Baptist Union decided they could no longer support the College. Efforts were made to persuade the City to assume the financial obligation, but Mayor Cater could not be swayed. The Baptist Union continued the struggle to maintain the institution. In the spring of 1939 a bylaw was passed authorizing the City to levy one mill towards the support of the College. In the late 1950's grants from the Provincial Government and from the Canada Council permitted the College to start planning an ambitious expansion program.

In 1961 the J. R. C. Evans Lecture Theatre and the Arts Building, including the Library, were constructed. The following year saw the building of the Men's Residence, and in 1963 the Ladies' Residence and the Music Building were added. Work was started on the Education Building in 1966. If the Sixties marked a period of unrest among university students in this country, certainly the Brandon College Directors were not idly sitting out the revolution. They were planning the change to University status which was to take place in 1967.

The occasion for this photograph is the installation of the sixth president of Brandon College Inc., Dr. John E. Robbins, on January 6, 1961. He is shown, lower right, with W. F. McGregor and Dr. A. E. McKenzie, centre, who conducted the installation. Standing from L to R are other members of the Board of Directors: D. R. MacKay, G. P. Sutherland, and Milton C. Holden. Among the many notables attending the function was Olive Diefenbaker, a graduate of the College, who officially opened the J. R. C. Evans Lecture Theatre.

This Brandon College convocation parade, circa 1925, includes some prominent Brandon personalities: Christina McLeod, Lily Harrison, J. G. Smart, Alderman Reg Longworth, Dr. Doyle, J. R. Reid, and, second from R, Rev. Kelly Stone.

Somehow these two Brandon College students don't seem to have the ideal conditions for serious work. Perhaps it's the lack of elbow room, but there are some distractions.

Brandon College professors have occasionally been known to adopt a less than academic mien. We can identify Professor Wright of the School of Music, fourth in the back row.

Opportunity for schooling was made available to these children at Sioux Valley School when white settlement came to the West. "Back to basics", anyone?

This is Brandon's first school, built on the west side of Tenth Street in 1882. The front was brick and the rear portion lumber.

Recalling his early years in this school, Blake Winter, son of Brandon's second mayor, told of temperatures so low that year that thermometers placed outside the school windows kept breaking. After twelve instruments had been used, the school board refused to allow the purchase of any more. That winter the snowfall was very heavy and remained on the ground until late May.

This building still stands. The roof has been altered, and an addition of several feet has been added to the front, and the name Strathcona Block identifies it.

Here is Brandon School Board's first major building project after the construction of the Tenth Street school in 1882. Central School was built in 1892 on Sixth Street, within a year of the date of the calling of tenders. The hurried-up construction brought problems when the water pipes, placed only six feet below surface instead of nine, froze. This school also provided a high school department until 1907, when the Brandon Collegiate was erected on the adjoining lot.

First day to school is not a casual dress occasion for mother or for daughter in the spring of 1909. The young lady is Marjorie Trotter, daughter of Mr. and Mrs. Beecham Trotter whose home at 326 - 6th Street — Tintern — still bears that name. Marjorie and her mother are about to cross the street to Central School.

73

Here is part of Brandon's crop of teenagers in 1888, scions of some of our City's first families. Many were to become leaders in industry and in the professions, names such as Clement, Clendenning, Hooper, Matheson, and McKenzie, to name only a few.

This class of Grade Ten students at BCI, 1951-52, appears more relaxed than did their counterparts some sixty-odd years before. Of course, photography has something to do with it. The "in thing" for the guys here is such garb as draped pants, leather windbreakers, and easy shirt collars; the girls are literally less straight-laced.

Bob Coates, the teacher, had to check attendance on these forty-three kids twice a day. (Classrooms must have been larger then.) Ballpoint pens were just in, and quite messy; the students used hardback notebooks or tried to get away with using the ten-cent Jumbo.

"No, we don't like the colour of those bricks. Take 'em down!" is in essence what some City Council members said to the School Board when Brandon Collegiate was under construction in 1907. The bricks had been made by a local brick plant in which some of the Board members were said to have had an interest. The original building was finally completed with sixty-five thousand red bricks imported from Wisconsin. The school, with the later extension shown in this photo, is now an elementary-junior high school called New Era, thus named when the school in fact did start this new era in its history.

Alexandra School served the south side of Brandon for close to seventy years before it crumbled under the wrecker's ball in 1974. The first structure (with the portico) was built in 1906 at a cost of $24,750. Three extensions were subsequently added within five years as the school population rose.

Some will undoubtedly recall a frightening incident which occurred during the early Forties when a team of horses broke away from an ice wagon and ran amok through the playground. One child suffered a concussion.

There appears to be little evidence of stress among these teachers at Alexandra School, circa 1950. Some had come on staff as early as 1928 when a letter from the Superintendent to women applicants for teaching positions informed them that "The Brandon School Board has recently gone on record as strongly disapproving of smoking on the part of lady teachers while engaged on their staff. Your acceptance of the enclosed agreement will be taken as indicating that you are prepared to co-operate with the Board in this way for the purpose of setting a good example to the pupils." The directive was short-lived.

Here is the staff at Alexandra School in 1916. Six years later a number of these teachers were to be among the eighty-eight released from their jobs in the so-called "Teachers' Strike". The Board had passed a motion to reduce teachers' salaries by twenty-five percent for the last two months of the school term, with the alternative of the termination of the teachers' contracts. A letter to the Board signed by the teachers stated that they were willing to complete the school year at their present salaries provided the Board would rescind its motion. This the Board refused to do and the end of April, 1922 brought the termination of all teachers' contracts. During the remaining two months of the school year, classes were at first supervised by trustees, parents, and senior students until qualified persons could be hired. Not one of the former teachers was re-engaged when the next school year started. Some were

later to gain eminence as educators in other parts of the province.

Recognition for at least twenty-five years of teaching service in Brandon schools was initiated by the Brandon School Board in 1967. Henry Nordin, veteran educator, holds his tray on which is inscribed his period of service — 1928 to 1967. Also receiving recognition are: (Back row, L to R) J. J. Hill; Margaret Collins; Joseph Federick; Daisy (Carswell) Hildebrand; Isabelle McGregor; Irving Bateman; Winnifred Greaves; William Peden; Lillian Popkin; (Front row) Thelma Schreiner; Kenneth Burgess, Chairman of Brandon School District No. 129; Mr. Nordin; Laura Bedford; Margaret Doak. Later the same year when Brandon School Division No. 40 was formed, Mr. Hill was appointed Superintendent of Schools.

This building has provided educational opportunity for hundreds of young men and women in Western Manitoba. Built in 1913 at a cost of $500,000, the Normal School graduated teachers for over a quarter of a century. The last teachers to be trained in this school graduated in 1940, and the building was turned over to the Military for the duration of the war. Unsuccessful efforts were made to have the teacher training program returned. It finally became the Agricultural Extension Centre and now provides accommodation and meeting facilities for education- and agriculture-related workshops and meetings.

This is the construction crew that built the Normal School. At one point work was interrupted due to a strike over wages.

The youngsters in this grade two class at David Livingstone School are in "position one" as they listen to the first Manitoba Schools Art broadcast, "It's fun to draw", on May 16, 1947. The kids will, hopefully, have their fun later. Their teacher is Florence (Baker) Endall.

August 25, 1951 was a red-letter day for John Chudzik. Why wouldn't he be laughing — apart from the fact that Mrs. Kate Aitken is giving him a hug? He's just had his first airplane ride and an all-expenses-paid visit to the Canadian National Exhibition in Toronto. He is representing his grade five class back in David Livingstone School, Brandon, to receive the prize awarded them for the best entry submitted from some 500 schools in a national mural competition.

King George School, built in 1911, has given way to a modern one-storey building whose final construction is being completed at this ceremony in 1979.

Young Darryl Lapensee, a kindergarten student, holds the ribbon which he and Mr. Rogerson are about to place in the time capsule that is to be embedded in the cornerstone. In the capsule the students have put such memorabilia as a set of coins, written accounts of what life was like in 1979, and school photographs and signatures.

Also participating in the ceremony are Principal Arnold Hersak and Superintendent Les Milne, holding the time capsule.

Mr. Rogerson had been a grade one student when the first King George School opened.

Of Brandon's first school on Tenth Street, people said in the 1880's that it had not been properly planned, it was badly lighted, and it had poor ventilation. It did not last long as a school.

Brandon's most recently-built school, Riverheights, was opened almost one hundred years later, in 1980. Built well into the ground, the school's heating, lighting, and air control systems are carefully monitored to ensure maximum energy efficiency.

The students of Riverheights are watching the ceremony of placing the time capsule into the cornerstone, the last step in the completion of the school in 1980.

Identified in the picture at the extreme left is Harold Tripp, Custodian; Secretary Rita Cullen assists Ian Goldstone and an unidentified student in preparing the capsule. At the right are Principal Harold Stewart and James Cornett.

This first meeting of the Union of Manitoba Municipalities, held March 15, 1905, among other recommendations, promoted the concept of government ownership of all telephone lines. Brandon Mayor Fleming was its first president.

The "Voice of the Brandon Winter Fair" has just told another of his hilarious jokes, for which he was renowned during his more than twenty years of emceeing at fairs throughout western Canada. "Dick" Painter was associated with the Federal Department of Agriculture during the Thirties and Forties and travelled through the West advising farmers on the control of grasshopper and warble fly infestations.

"You find the farmers at the fairs," he said; and that's where he found Alex McPhail (L) and Jim Moffatt (R), secretary and president respectively of the Manitoba Winter Fair in 1957.

This photo shows Brandon's first Winter Fair Board, circa 1908. These men of vision developed an institution that has since made Brandon, Manitoba internationally known for its Royal Manitoba Winter Fair. From L to R they are James McQueen, J. D. McGregor, Joseph Cornell, L. L. Harwood, Robert Hall, Charles Fraser, W. Warren, G. R. Coldwell, J. W. Fleming.

This log dwelling was once home for James Duncan McGregor, an early Brandon pioneer who in 1929 was appointed to the highest office in the province, the Lieutenant-Governor of Manitoba. His promotion of improving breeding of cattle brought him international recognition. It has been said that no Brandon citizen has ever achieved the general popularity of this man.

Symbolically, the message of this open door is that, regardless of what is left behind, opportunity awaits the taker.

This Avro 548 is about to leave Winnipeg for Brandon with a packet of *Tribunes*. The date is July 28, 1921.

Aviation became a reality in Brandon in September of 1929 when a group of interested citizens obtained a charter to establish the Brandon Aero Association. They sold shares at $100 each and purchased some acreage on First Street North. They acquired an Avro Avion biplane, engaged a young flyer from Winnipeg, W. A. Catton, as flying instructor and air engineer, and were in business. The venture folded in 1934, but a year later a new group established The Brandon Flying Club, with C. E. Leech as its first president.

The Club gained such a favourable reputation for the high calibre of pilots it was turning out that it was selected the first club in Canada to train pilots for the Royal Canadian Air Force. In the summer of 1939 the first class of trainees arrived, and the Tiger Moths shown in this photo were the first aircraft used. Later, when the British Commonwealth Air Training Station was established five miles north of the Club's field, civil flying operations had to be suspended until after the war.

The first Provisional Pilot Officers to be trained in Brandon for the Royal Canadian Air Force in 1939 are shown here with their instructors C. E. Leech, left and "Mac" McLean, right.

Two members of this class distinguished themselves in the Battle of Britain during World War II. Squadron leader "Bob" Morrow of Toronto and Vancouver, centre, was leader of the Hurri-Bomber Squadron that made low-level surprise attacks on railway and factory sites in northern France as well as on enemy convoys. Morrow designed a means of attaching two 250-pound delayed action bombs to the underside of the Hurricane wings. The entire squadron could then release their loads without danger of being caught in the explosions of the first bombs. Retaliation by anti-aircraft was ineffective on these raids due to their suddenness and the low level at which the planes flew.

Wing Commander "Granny" Morris from Oakville, Ontario, at Morrow's left, was decorated for shooting down three enemy aircraft and damaging another in the space of half an hour in night fighting over England. Both received the Distinguished Flying Cross.

John Ballinger is at Leech's left.

When the Flying Club resumed operations after the war, Ed McGill became Instructor-Manager of operations. This class of air cadets, shown with their instructors, graduated in the early Sixties.

# IV    The Wheat City

Countless photographs have been taken of farming operations in the decades since Robert Matheson, a young lawyer, coined the sobriquet "The Wheat City" to describe his home town a few years after 1882. Just a very few of the early harvest scenes are included in these pages. Hopefully, they will prompt the reader to ask a senior friend or relative to recall the days when the threshing outfits, behemoths of the harvest, dominated rural life from August until well after the first autumn frost. No one in his right mind would want to revert to the farming methods of those days; yet, one can almost detect a smile of self-satisfaction in the faces of the men and women who lived and toiled through those years when Wheat was King.

This wood-burning engine served a threshing outfit on a farm along the Valley Road. The gentlemen in the black fedoras and white collars obviously do not plan to roll up their sleeves and lend a hand.

There is nothing better than having a portable milk bar brought to the threshing location. Women have been said to be the heroines of the harvest, putting in at least as many hours as the men. Up before dawn to cook breakfast for the crew, they then prepared vegetables, and baked bread, biscuits, cakes, and pies for the day's meals. As well, they took lunches to the men at mid-morning and mid-afternoon. Other farm chores, such as the one shown in this picture, also had to be attended to.

Very early in Brandon's history grain elevators dominated the skyline. This photo, taken in 1887, shows wheat marketing in Brandon on Pacific Avenue. Brandon district wheat fields produced a bumper crop that year.

One early settler, N. J. King, kept a diary in which he made frequent entries during the winter telling about taking a load of wheat, in bags, to the elevators in Brandon. When weather was favourable, he would make several trips a week. The elevators provided bags for the farmers' use.

*Grain Blockade at Alexander Man March 3rd 1888 CPR Main Line*

Grain blockades in western Canada were not rare during the 1800's. The railways did not allow loading of grain from flat warehouses or from wagons, thereby placing private grain-handling companies in a monopoly position. A Royal Commission appointed in 1889 recommended that railways permit the building of flat warehouses, and that they provide platforms at shipping points. These recommendations were incorporated by The Manitoba Grain Act of 1900. This photo was taken at Alexander, Manitoba, on March 3, 1888 on the CPR Main Line.

Apart from this clutch of buildings and bags, the landscape is desolate.

85

Mills and McPhail own this outfit that is threshing on the grounds of the Provincial Asylum in Brandon, 1890.

Staying on top of your work is part of being a successful farmer. The huge "muffin" at the left will soon be ready for the separator to move in and thresh this field's crop.

This steam-driven threshing outfit was used before 1900 on a farm not far from Brandon. Hauling water for the Case steamer and for the crew was a full-time job.

Jim Thompson, seated atop the giant wheel, and Archie Rae, holding aloft a sheaf of wheat, are the only two identified in this photo.

Two or three men are kept busy filling, sewing up, and loading the grain bags. If the wind was from an unfavourable direction, this job could be the dirtiest in the harvesting operation. The men would sometimes wear necker-chiefs to prevent straw from getting into their shirts.

The Kirkham outfit shown here was one of the big ones at the turn of the century.

To choose the ideal location for threshing one had to be a prognosticator. What side of the barn would be the best location? Was there the likelihood of a wind shift? What does the Almanac say? During such an operation as this one there was always a chance of a spark starting a fire. The ground had to be wetted to avoid this possibility.

One of the Kirkham daughters came to visit the outfit on her new-fangled contraption, a lady's bicycle. The appearance of this vehicle in Western Canada threatened even the horse. The *Winnipeg Weekly Times*, July 4, 1882, said of the early models: "The bicyclist upon the highway is a moving menace to the public peace. He frightens horses, runs down small boys and elderly ladies... it is justifiable to shoot him on sight."

Wheat straw was put to good use in building cabins for pigs at the Dominion Experimental Farm from about 1890 till the mid-Thirties.

Hydroelectric power drives this thresher on the Patterson farm circa 1906.

They are either too old or too young to help with the threshing, but Grandfather and the young lad have come to watch the operation.

The Gaar Scott engine and separator, circa 1908, are part of the J. Dixon threshing outfit shown here. The smoke stack cap is a spark arrestor. The tractor appears to be much like the engine that went over the edge of the First Street Bridge ramp in 1925.

"Bundling" in this scene refers, of course, to the gathering up of the stooks of grain. The young ladies don't appear to be involved in the actual harvesting operation. But how can one be sure? It was wartime; there might well have been a shortage of manpower. And as to dress — it was not customary for women to wear more practical garb in 1916.

During the Thirties gophers as well as grasshoppers made havoc of the grain fields. The municipality suffering a gopher infestation provided the poison that would be mixed with grain and spread around the gopher holes. Here we have a gopher gang about to start on an expedition to the grain fields.

Municipalities also paid a bounty of one cent to five cents on gophers. Kids made their spending money catching gophers with snares and traps. Municipal clerks can recall with some revulsion, no doubt, having a sack of not-so-fresh gopher tails dumped on their desks by a youngster who expected an immediate count of his bag.

The neighbours said it would never work but George Stott, on the Lauson tractor, and George Butler, on the Nicholson Shepard combine, proved them wrong. This photo was taken in 1936.

Field day brought out this large group of Brandon area farmers in the summer of 1931. They have an opportunity to examine and discuss the quality of a stand of wheat.

The Manitoba Farm Boys' Camp was a regular feature at the Provincial Exhibition until about 1940. The fellows had about three days of intensive instruction related to all branches of farming and practice in judging grain and livestock, with some recreation on the side.

Here is the 1935 camp.

After the Second World War boys' and girls' club activity was renewed in the 4-H movement. Brandon Exhibition hosted 4-H rallies for some twenty years. This handful of grain is getting some pretty serious consideration.

Who wouldn't look happy about selling two dozen eggs for a cool $1000? Cheryl Macpherson is the young lady holding the Manitoba Egg Producers Marketing Board's trophy for the junior producer class at the Manitoba Winter Fair in 1977. Ed Hutsal, representing the buyer, Feed Rite Limited, is holding the fragile five hundred dollar package.

This photo shows a small section of some 2000 4-H club members assembled for the ceremony of the opening of the new 4-H building at the Provincial Exhibition grounds on July 2, 1962. George Hutton, Manitoba's Minister of Agriculture, performed the honours. Ninety clubs in colourful uniforms and bearing their club banners then paraded around the racetrack to the grandstand for the presentation of awards.

# V    The Horse Capital of Canada

Automobile dealers in the 1980's are rarely, if ever, the object of the church minister's admonition to desist from selling a "lemon" for fear of the wrath of the Almighty. The counterpart of the car salesman in the 1880's, the horse dealer, was frequently and perhaps with just cause warned from the pulpit to refrain from making unscrupulous dealings.

During the first three decades of Brandon's history the horse was king, both in town and county. To the first settlers who started farming with oxen, acquiring at least one team of horses was an early priority. The first horses often worked alongside a team of oxen, but eventually the farmer's aspiration of owning several horses became a reality. In the city the livery stable rented out horse-drawn vehicles to those who did not keep their own.

Brandon was the ideal location for horseman and prospective buyer to make a deal. One of Brandon's early horsemen, Beecham Trotter, travelled to Scotland, France, and Belgium to personally select the horses he knew would be bought by Manitoba farmers.

Among the owners of the three dominant breeds, the Clydesdale, the Percheron, and the Belgian, there was keen rivalry at the horse fairs. Tensions comparable to those at a crucial hockey game prevailed during the judging competitions. The announcement of the judges' decision was greeted by wild cheering from the benches of the winning breed's supporters.

Brandon in 1886 had twenty-three livery stables and about as many horse dealers, thereby deserving its title of "The Horse Capital of Canada".

By 1891, Brandon was known as the horse trading centre of the west. Before the Winter Fair was organized, "The Stallion Show" was held in the fall of the year.

This one is in the city square, probably 1891, as construction of the City Hall appears to be almost completed. The official opening is to take place February 29, 1892.

For many years at the summer fairs, prior to the evening performance, the grandstand audience was treated to the livestock parade at least once during Fair Week. This photo shows the 1898 parade getting under way.

These two bovine stars appear completely undaunted by all the attention they are getting. Could this have been an entry in one of the countless parades that are part of Brandon's history? The date is 1904.

As early as 1912 the United Commercial Travellers were keenly interested in supporting Brandon fairs. Later they and the Associated Canadian Travellers joined to sponsor the gala Travellers' Day Parade that is still an exciting part of Fair week.

Carefully matched teams of horses were shown at a long line of Winter Fairs held in the Arena at Tenth and Victoria. These horses are owned by the T. Eaton Company, and are a reminder of the times when home deliveries were made by horse-drawn van.

This six-horse team exhibit from Elton Municipality at the 1912 Fair, is advertising the International Brotherhood of Teamsters, Local 332: "We are united to protect; not combined to injure. Come and join us." Owners of teams are Duncan and Jack McCallum, and Alex Forsyth. The white canvas bunny-ear hats protect the horses from flies.

In answer to gas rationing during World War II, Archie MacArthur, Sr., of MacArthur Transportation, put two teams in Winnipeg and three teams in Brandon to deliver freight. From 1942 to 1949, six-horse teams of Clydesdales were shown throughout the "A" fair circuit, and at local "B" fairs as well. Against a background of Machinery Row and the "new" grandstand (built in 1912), George MacArthur and son Jim are ready to show at the 1946 Provincial Exhibition.

John Stott's Percheron is being shown here. Until 1903, only the Clydesdale breed was shown at Brandon Fairs. Gradually, Perchersons and Belgians increased in popularity until, by 1940, Percherons registered in Canada outnumbered registered Clydesdales.

Horsemen, cattlemen, and the general public are attracted to the sales ring by the auctioneer's lilting jargon and the ringmen's exuberant shouts. Excitement is high in the pervading stillness of the crowd, where the shake of a paper or the nod of a head could make one the new owner of a 1,500-pound bull during this 1978 Bull Sale at the Brandon Winter Fair.

Kids' riding is part of the Royal Winter Fair. Here Mrs. Lillyon Isaacs of Winnipeg is presenting a plaque to the Chiswell children for their participation in the show.

The Arena and Winter Fair Building, as viewed from McTavish Avenue, boasted fireproof barns built in 1921 to replace the ones lost in the 1920 fire.

A "drag race", 1882 version, is about to start at the corner of Rosser Avenue and Eighth Street. Many tales are told of illicit racing on Rosser in the early days, but this race appears to be in order. Dr. Fleming's drug store provides grandstand accommodation at the right.

It's "time out" from the routine work of the horse show for the Horseman's Hoedown. Nestor Lombaert, fiddler, is accompanied on guitar by S. E. Bennett. Wilbur Rice of Binscarth and Fred Dunn, Alexander, seem to have an ear for music. The chaps in the broom and bucket brigade are unidentified.

The grandstands are full and there
is standing room only at this
Summer Fair at the turn of the
century. The next race is about to
start.

Not too much has changed in
forty years. The excitement of the
race is still here, but there is a
new grandstand and the jockeys
now wear silks. Somehow, the
crowds seem to have diminished.

Horse racing continued to be
popular feature of the Provincial
Exhibition until the grandstand was
demolished in the early 1970's.
This view of the Exhibition Grounds
looks toward the south.

Through the years, the jumping
horses have performed for
appreciative Brandon Fair spectators. Here, Ted Rowe is up, at the
1904 horse show.

The era of the jumping horse reached its zenith with the advent of "Bouncing Buster" who, through well over a decade, thrilled admiring Brandon and Western Canada fair-goers with his smooth grace and apparent ease in clearing the hurdles. He was owned by Lilla-Gord Stables and ridden only by Lil or Gordon Williamson, unless a junior rider was stipulated in the class. From summer, 1941 at the Brandon Exhibition to at least 1954, Bouncing Buster won a mind-boggling number of trophies, ribbons, and championships. Showman that he was, he sulked and jumped badly if the crowd was small, but he performed flawlessly when the hushed awe followed by tumultuous appreciation of a large audience was forthcoming. He jumped only as high as he needed to clear the fence. At Boissevain in 1946, that proved to be an exhibition of jump of 6 feet 2 inches. In the Knock-down-and-out class at the Calgary Spring Show of 1945, he cleared sixty-two fences in order to win.

Buster was eleven years old when he started "bouncing" for Lilla-Gord. Although the prophets predicted each to be "his last year", spring, 1954 saw Bouncing Buster take home the J. G. Patterson Memorial Trophy, denoting champion jumper of the Calgary Show. To date, no jumping horse in Brandon history has come close to the record set by Bouncing Buster.

Among these directors of the Provincial Exhibition, 1894, are eminent horsemen.

At the Dominion Experimental Farm in 1890 early harvesting operations are under way. Horses provide some of the power needed to get this crop off.

The home of the first superintendent, S. A. Bedford, overlooks this pleasant scene.

Horses were the power behind all farm operations in the early days. This man, with his team of Clydesdales, has just hauled out a sleighload of poplar, which could be sawn into firewood lengths or used "as is" for building rail fences.

These 1910 "stars on ice" provided much-needed fuel for refrigeration until the 1940's, when hydroelectric power became available to all homes in the area. Ice blocks weighing fifty to one hundred pounds were hoisted out of the Assinboine River at Sixteenth Street, using ice tongs and crowbars, and were placed on the sleigh. The horses are blanketed against the cold and wear full harness, with breeching, for the heavy pull up the river bank.

An eight-horse tandem team powers this road grader, owned by the McRae Family of South Brandon, and driven by Jack McRae. The passengers are relatives from Scotland, out to seek their fortunes in the new land.

This array of lively horses gave worthy service to the City's Fire Department. They are shown here in front of Brandon's first Fire Hall, 1882 - 1911. The second floor of this building held the Civic Offices, the Council Chamber, and the Police Court. The prisoner cell was below.

The bell in the tower was placed there in 1902 to commemorate the coronation of King Edward VII. Weighing 4,400 pounds, it is made of 77 percent copper and 23 percent tin, and measures 62 inches across the base. It presently rests on the floor in No. 1 Firehall on Princess Avenue.

By 1912 Brandon had a new firehall on Princess Avenue, designed by Architect W. A. Elliott. This photo shows the new horse-drawn mechanized equipment. The horses are housed in the rear of the building, and within ten seconds of an alarm the equipment and the men are ready to go.

Fire Station No. 2 has served many other functions in its lifetime. During World War II it was used as an infirmary for No. 2 Manning Depot. It later became a manual training school, then a temporary home for the B. J. Hales Museum.

During the Sixties and Seventies it housed the Brandon School Division offices and Board Room.

Here is the interior of Fire Station No. 2. The equipment is ready for the horses to back into, and the harness drops down to be fastened on the horse in a matter of seconds.

A thirty-eight horsepower unit moved this house up Fifteenth Street at Louise Avenue in 1910.

Here is a troop of Brandon's own Royal North West Mounted Police Force that was stationed here in 1919-20. They are returning to their barracks at the Armouries following a horsemanship practice session. This photo shows them crossing the Little Saskatchewan River some miles north of Brandon.

Fast winter travel in pioneer days was possible with this trim cutter. Under that fur robe the gentlemen probably have a heated stone or sadiron to keep their feet warm.

The Pitfield family is about to start off on an outing in the democrat. Horses could make good time pulling this kind of vehicle.

Early Brandon claimed more livery stables per city block than any place in the world. In 1912 one could ride in high style in Weir's Livery Brougham. By 1918 the establishment had entered the motorized era, and advertised as follows: "Weir's Auto Livery always open. Taxi and touring car; careful drivers."

Reminiscent of "the good old days" is this elegant vehicle carrying four elegant ladies of the Brandon Council of Women. Mrs. Effie McPhail and Mrs. Flora Cowan can be identified at the left. This imposing entrance gate, one of the last structures of the great era of the Brandon Fair-that-was, was torn down around 1968.

The Thirties forced innovations in people's lifestyles. With pocket-books thin, farmers were forced to give up driving their cars. Here is one version of the Bennett Buggy, 1934.

This school bus of the 1930's would be put on sleigh runners for winter, and probably had a wood-burning heater installed for added comfort.

These youngsters are enjoying the annual Boxing Day sleigh ride in Cumming and Dobbie's two-horse open sleigh which, for the rest of the winter, delivers coal to Brandon homes. Here is Gordon Cumming handling the team for the 1948 ride.

When the first horseless carriage appeared in Brandon in 1903, the king of transportation, the mighty Clydesdale, had no inkling as to the implication this contraption would have on his future. William Muir must have cut a dash when he first drove down Sixth Street in this vehicle.

In 1925 when this photo was taken, Mrs. Baldock (left) appears to know what should get this iron beast going. It would not have been unusual, however, if she had had to go back to get a team of horses to complete the job she set out to do.

That horse is not going to move until someone gets that four-wheeled motorized contraption out of the way.

At the Canadian National Express building behind the Prince Edward Hotel, District Superintendent Carl Palmer (left), William Butler, Rod Chambers, and an unidentified gentleman with the horse and buggy await the arrival of the CNR train.

Horse and buggy, automobile, and streetcar vie for supremacy at the corner of Tenth and Rosser.

# VI The Garden City of the Golden West

" . . . There is . . . a cool breeze blowing, so that it does not seem so bad if you can get in the shade to work; but that is impossible unless it is under a tent, or in a house or the shade of one, for there is not a tree about here large enough for a cow to rub against." This excerpt from a letter written from Brandon on July 17, 1881 by William Orchard to his family in England hardly describes a "Garden City"; yet the city would deserve the name before twenty years had passed. Brandon residents showed an early interest in planting shade trees and shrubs on their property, and in cultivating beautiful garden plots. Horticultural fairs were well attended even by 1898. Interest in maintaining beautiful home grounds and parks has never waned, so that the name "Garden City" endures today even as it did at the turn of the century.

Home life for a Sioux Indian family early in the century still centred around this carefully crafted teepee.

Visitors have just arrived at this sod home. Pioneers tell of having cattle housed adjacent to the dwelling to help keep the home heated.

These two fellows appear to be fairly content with their lot. The log house with sod roof was a first habitation.

Mrs. Rutherford, travelling to Brandon in 1882, stayed overnight in such a place. She says in a letter: "At that time in Brandon there was only a small wooden shed for a station and some tents.... We put off at a side place where we had to walk three miles to a friend of Willie's where we were to stay the night. We were glad to get into a place where we would get a bed. It came on an awful thunderstorm and the rain came down the roof and into the beds, and the mud running down the walls, for in those days there was nothing but log houses plastered with mud, which is well enough in winter when we have no rain, but when the fresh comes in the spring it makes an awful mess."

This Victorian mansion is the J. C. Kavanagh home, circa 1889. Mr. Kavanagh was Brandon's first postmaster.

The "Half-way House", the Weir family home twelve miles northeast of Brandon, was one of many such places in the rural parts, giving overnight accommodation to weary travellers in the 1880's.

The windmill, which was the first form of mechanized power on Manitoba farms, preceded both the horse-drawn sweep and the treadmill in pioneer agriculture.

A very new invention in 1882, a bicycle, is leaning against the house.

Here are the old and the new on the McPherson homestead in the Brandon Hills.

Those who can recall the arduous chore of making butter with a dasher in the crock can appreciate the look of boredom on this woman's face. Only the end result can compensate for the tedium of the task.

Tackling Monday's wash does not quell this young lady's apparent happiness. And why should it? Her laundry is well-equipped with a wringer washer, the wringer being movable from the machine to the tub stand. The copper boiler at the corner can be used to boil those household linens that must have that whiter than white look. And someone else is slaving over a hot stove while she enjoys the best of air conditioning.

The kind-faced woman in this photo is Mrs. Dougald McVicar, the first postmistress of Grand Valley and the one who gave that place its name, September 12, 1879. It is from her recollections of pioneer life here that some of the early history of our city has been recorded. All the experiences of the early pioneer days have been engraved in her memory. This photograph was taken in her ninety-first year, 1941.

The home of Brandon's first mayor, T. Mayne Daly, was at the corner of Rosser Avenue and Eighteenth Street. This historical building has been refurbished by the Assiniboine Historical Society and now houses a museum collection typical of the furnishings of a home at the turn of the century. 'n one of the rooms, the furniture of the former city council chambers has been set up. The lowest level of the building contains equipment and some furnishings of a dentist's office, a butcher shop, and Mutter's store. The archive is located on the third floor.

This obviously is the kitchen.

CITY OF BRANDON

VISIT OF GOVENOR GENERAL EARL GREY
AT HOME OF SENATOR KIRKHOFFER
1909

The house at 247 Russell Street saw, early in the century, a social life parallel to that in the most elevated circles in Ottawa. Senator and Mrs. Kirkhoffer entertained such personages as HRH the Duke of York and, in this photo, Canada's Governor-General Earl Grey. Their daughter Kathleen, when in her teens, would occasionally don a cap and apron to do the service of a maid, then later resume her proper role as daughter, unbeknownst to the distinguished guests.

This is a real Power house, with seven of the eight Power sisters taking part in some shenanigans. Dressed her in father's garb at left is the youngest daughter, Laura. The other girls, from left, are Rhoda (Tennant), who was the first woman to be elected to Brandon City Council, Beth, Edna, Verta, Levina, and Violet. The eighth sister had just recently been married so is not included here.

Mr. Power had been manager of Kelly House, one of Brandon's earlier hotels, until he and his wife decided to take up farming north of the city.

Synonymous with the beauty of Brandon's generously shaded streets is the name Patmore. When the city was little more than bald prairie, Henry Lewis Patmore, shown here, arrived from England in 1883, and soon afterward joined the staff of the Brandon Experimental Farm. Here he experimented with different trees and shrubs to develop strains that could tolerate the extremes of Manitoba's seasons.

Graceful ascending elm trees, a species developed by his son, R.H. "Dick" Patmore, adorn the boulevards on Clark Drive, making that street one of the most beautiful in the city.

The Seed Selection Special has just pulled into the CPR Depot, circa 1905. Coming in the dead of winter, the train carries a staff of agricultural specialists who give lectures about farming methods, and discuss the suitability of particular grains for western farms.

Later trains, called the *Horticultural Show on Wheels*, gave far more information. They carried displays of floral arrange-ments as well as produce grown from various kinds of seeds. They illustrated advantages of particular types of shrubs and trees for specific regions, and in all cases told the potential customers where they might order the product.

The horticultural staff lived on the trains during the scheduled run. Brandon agronomists from the Experimental Farm were frequently invited to travel to points west to assist in the lectures.

118

This photo, taken about 1905-10, shows the residence of the Superintendent at the Brandon Experimental Farm. The house, built in the 1890's, is identical to those built at the first five stations across Canada.

It's apple picking time — not in the Okanagan — but in Brandon, Manitoba at the Experimental Farm in 1929.

Here are the results of scientific agriculture. This wagon load of turnips is being harvested at the Dominion Experimental Farm, circa 1920.

The Government of Canada Research Station receives hundreds of visitors every year. This group of Women's Institute members is making a stopover at the Station during a tour in 1952.

Not at all pretentious, but adequate, is this home in Brandon. With the blue and amber glass on the front porch, the bit of gingerbread on the roof, and the verandah, it is typical of hundreds of comfortable homes in Brandon during the 1920's.

Trees like the ones shading this stately home were not a part of the landscape in the 1880's. This residence is at Twelfth and Louise.

This sturdy rental complex, Lorne Terrace, was built by Hughes and Company early in the century and remains their property. It was considered in 1919 as a suitable officers' barracks and dwelling for the RNWMP but the disastrous fire in the Police horse barns late that year put an end to all plans to stay in Brandon.

Brandon is a city of beautiful gardens, but not all are as visible for public appreciation and enjoyment as is this one at the Hendzel home on Rosser Avenue. "Gus" Hendzel was known to thousands of households through his very practical gardening column in the *Brandon Sun*.

Here is a view of Helen Hendzel's garden, a perennial prize winner in the Brandon Horticultural Society's home grounds competition.

By 1926 when this photo was taken, more and more people had cars to take them away on their summer vacations. This is Brandon's first tourist motel.

The members of the Horticultural Society proposed a tree-planting ceremony in Jubilee Park in Brandon's west end to commemorate the coronation of King George VI and Queen Elizabeth on May 12, 1937. Accordingly, trees were planted by organizations or individuals in honour of some Brandon person, and carved stone plaques still identify the trees.

This cairn was provided by these citizens, some of whom can be identified: (counting from L to R) 1. W. B. Bain   3. W. N. Sutherland   5. Mary McGuinness 6. George Dinsdale   7. Rev. J. E. Bell.

With the dedication of the cairn, the park became known as Coronation Park. In the ceremony of dedication these words were part of the litany: "Thou shalt not destroy the trees by forcing an axe against them. And thou shalt not cut them down for the tree of the field is man's life."

These full-grown trees in the park at the Exhibition Grounds shelter this building which was moved here about 1928. In the foreground is the "dog's drinking fountain" designed to allow man and his best friend to have a drink together.

The building is the original McLaren School, built in 1917 on Second Street in the South End.

Just south of the present Brandon Recreational Centre lies this rare tract of land once called Bang's Bush, but now more generally known as John Indian's Bush. Why "rare"? This is possibly the last piece of prairie land that has eluded the city developer. Some three years ago (1978) the land, still the property of the City, was seriously considered for a housing project, but the objections to this proposal were sufficient to persuade the City to leave this bit of original prairie as a park area. Lawrence Stuckey, a member of the local Natural History Society, catalogued some eighty-eight species of flowering plants, twelve species of trees, and a great variety of wildlife in the area. This unique piece of land might well remain as one of the few existing links between generations past and those to come.

# VII   Pearl of the Prairies

Brandon has always enjoyed a rich and varied cultural life unmatched by many larger and wealthier cities. Partly a consequence of its relative isolation from metropolitan centres, this cultural activity has long involved a wide cross-section of the community: church groups, the university, the schools, service clubs, ethnic organizations, community drama groups, the art club, the women's musical club to name only a few.

While recordings and television have now largely replaced the grand tours, Brandon has been visited at one time or another by almost every major soloist and performing ensemble. Dame Nellie Melba, Harry Lauder, Grace Fields, Alex Templeton, Percy Grainger, Thomas L. Thomas, Jan Peerce, Byron Janis, Lois Marshall, Steicher and Horowitz, the Minneapolis Symphony Orchestra, Catherine McKinnon, Dinah Christie, Dave Broadfoot, and Don Harron are names which will suggest the richness of opportunities Brandonites have had to experience artistic genius at first hand.

Earlier audiences thrilled to the annual visits of the great Chautauqua tent with its smorgasbord of performers; later audiences have applauded the merits of the Royal Winnipeg Ballet, the Winnipeg Symphony Orchestra, the Confederation Centre's *Anne of Green Gables*, and Les Feux Follets. Earlier audiences went to the movies at the Bijou, the Starland, or the Empire, or attended vaudeville shows at the Capital. Later audiences have found stimulation at Mosaic Massey, the festival of life and learning which has brought to Brandon such prominent speakers and entertainers as Marshall McLuhan, Buckminster Fuller, Alvin Toffler, Ralph Nader, Madame Benoit, Leona Boyd, Al Purdy, Dorothy Livesay, W. O. Mitchell, Roy Bonisteel, Paul Martin, Barbara Frum, Knowlton Nash, Lloyd Robertson, Al Oeming, Earle Birney, and Anton Kuerti.

This satisfying blend of the local and the national and the international has made Brandon truly one of the most stimulating cities in which to live and raise a family, stimulating far beyond what simple population statistics would suggest.

This elegant home of yesteryear, the former John E. Smith residence, presently serves as Brandon's Art Centre. On the main floor are the gallery, the office of the Allied Arts Council, and a ballet classroom. Painting studios are located on the second floor and pottery workrooms are in the basement.

Brandon women have long concerned themselves with more than home duties. The Brandon Council of Women sponsored winter courses on a variety of subjects: parliamentary procedure, finances for women, and the pleasures of leisure, just to name a few — and all well before the International Women's Year created a greater awareness of women in society.

These are the women of the 1958 winter course.

The desire to share their appreciation of the beautiful was sufficiently strong in this prairie city back in 1907 to prompt a group of some thirty women to organize the Brandon Art Club (BAC). Wives of business and professional men, as well as career women such as nurses and teachers, formed the greater portion of the early membership. Within a very few years membership had jumped to 200, necessitating their using the dining room of the Prince Edward Hotel for their Saturday afternoon meetings.

Art education in the public schools as well as instructive art lectures for the general public were among the projects they supported. They encouraged local musicians and artists, and created an awareness of the arts of new Canadians by arranging displays of old world handwork. They established, as well, a library of over 100 carefully selected books on the arts.

The Presidents of the BAC from 1907 to 1957 are assembled here to mark their fifty years' anniversary. Back row, L to R: Mrs. G. R. Rowe, Miss Marjorie McKenzie, Mrs. D. R. Doig, Mrs. Joseph Donaldson, Mrs. Barney Thordarson; front row: Mrs. J. R. C. Evans, Mrs. W. A. Bigelow, Mrs. Robert A. (Madge) Clement (founding president), Mrs. J. E. Matthews, Mrs. S. J. S. Pierce, Mrs. Malcolm McGregor.

The first Manitoba Music Educators' Workshop was held February 24 and 25, 1961 and featured performances by a massed choir of teachers from across the province and two orchestras of students from throughout the province. Conductors brought to Brandon for the early workshops included Victor Feldbrill, John Strohm, Richard Condie of the Mormon Tabernacle Choir, Harry Robert Wilson of Columbia University, Dr. Wilfrid Pelletier of the Metropolitan Opera, Clayton Krehbiel of the Cleveland Orchestra, Brian Priestman, and Albert Pratz. Shown at an organizational meeting are, L to R: Betty Knowlton, Chairman David Wilson, Robert Blair, Myna Magee, and Colin Mailer.

"A Glimpse of Yesteryear", a film depicting some of Brandon's early history, was produced as a project of the city's Manitoba Centennial Committee back in 1969.

Shown here is the Brandon Pioneer Committee that was charged to make the arrangements for the production. From L to R they are: Rev. Earl S. Dixon, Betty Hatch, Tully McKenzie, S. Rosenman, D Brown, Mrs. E. McPhail, Mrs. Hoare.

126

Women in the Red Cross Society show here some of the activity in which they were involved during World War II — sewing, knitting, and quilting.

St. John Ambulance workers faithfully attend large public functions to render emergency first aid when required. One such volunteer, George J. Oliver, shown in this photo seated at the right, was admitted in May of 1953 to the Order of St. John of Jerusalem by sanction of Her Majesty Queen Elizabeth II. Mr. Oliver was awarded the Military Medal for gallantry at Vimy and also the Distinguished Conduct Medal.

Giving a hand to worthwhile projects is not limited to older people by any means. These lads show that they can have fun while working on a very worthwhile project — making bird-houses to entice the bluebird to return to the prairie region. The boys are shown with the founder of the Brandon Junior Birders Club, Dr. John Lane. Well over 3,000 bird-houses have been strung out along the highways and country roads in the Western Manitoba region alone.

The annual visit of the circus has always been a highlight of the year for many Brandonites. In earlier years, the circus grounds just east of Sixth Street above Victoria housed the big tents of such circus greats as Barnum and Bailey, and Clyde Beatty. In more recent years, the Keystone has been the site for the Shrine Circus and the pre-circus show featuring the local Car Patrol, Pipes and Drums, and the colourful Oriental Band pictured here.

Once upon a time almost every town and village had a bandstand in the park and a town band to give concerts. Here is Brandon Citizens' Band of 1907.

Bands travelled fair distances to play in competitions with other town bands. Alexander, for example, had an excellent band in 1932; so did Portage la Prairie. The big contest was, of course, at Brandon Fair, when the competing bands would play to a full grandstand.

The musicians usually supplied their own instruments, and the City provided the uniforms. The City Band was expected to play for official functions and in parades. They did give a hoot, and all for free, of course.

If there's a Scottish program in Brandon you can be sure it's a sellout. Some fifty years ago, the feeling of the skirl of the pipes was even more intense. It prompted a group of citizens of Scottish origin to organize a boys' pipe band in 1934 and to engage an instructor from Scotland. A Ladies' Auxiliary held whist drives and Scottish nights to raise money to buy the chanters.

Here is the first Brandon Boys' Pipe Band, splendidly decked out in their kilts. These kilts were discovered quite by accident in Park School. No one knew how they came to be there, but the School Board agreed that there was a far better use for them than remaining in storage.

Within a few years a number of these lads answered the call of another drum when World War II broke out. Some did not return.

From L to R, Back row: Doug Robertson, Bob Patterson, Charlie Creighton, Bernard Redman, Harold Creighton, Ewan Wallace. Centre row: Jim Summers, Don Manson, Bill Manson, Gordon Sinclair, Jim Reid, Norm Milne. Front row: Drum Major Bill Redman, Stirling Wallace, Ken Creighton, Pipe Major Jimmie Kay.

These youngsters dance to a different drum. Many will remember this performance at the Provincial Exhibition, circa 1970.

This quintet of Ukrainian musicians is about to play under the baton of Wasyl Bobyk. In the group are Mike Nazer, John Nazer, Luka Blanarovich, Paul ꞌmigelski. The chap at the right was just travelling through the city and he stopped over for a visit. He cannot be identified.

St. Augustine's Church and Monastery, on the corner of Fourth Street and Lorne Avenue, was constructed in three separate sections. The monastery in the foreground was begun in September, 1899 and completed in November of the same year as a home for the Redemptorist Fathers who had begun work in the parish in 1898. The cornerstone for the church (extreme left) was laid in June, 1902 and the church opened and consecrated in August, 1903. The church and monastery were joined in 1904 with the construction of the central section, originally used as an addition to the monastery; in 1924 it became the Parish School of St. Augustine's. It remained a school until 1962.

Methodists, in the persons of the Rev. Thomas Hall and Rev. Thomas Lawson, held some of the very first services in the Brandon district. The first mission was located on Sixth Street between Rosser and Princess, and the first church proper, shown here, was on Seventh Street between Lorne and Louise. Renovations to the building had just been completed when this photo was taken in 1895, and it was on this occasion that the minister, the Rev. Leonard Gaetz, predicted that before long there would have to be a still larger building "in which there would be no empty benches". By 1899 this prophecy was to become a reality. The adults in this photo are, L to R: Mrs. Adams, Mrs. Leech, Mrs. Van Tassel, Mrs. Ashley, Beecham Trotter, Mrs. Trotter, Rev. Gaetz, Mrs. Bodden, Rev. Darrel, J. Sproule, E. Bennest, D. Reesor, Mr. Bodden, T. Butcher.

In the Fifties and Sixties Brandon was finding how very inadequate its performance facilities had become in an age when Canada Council and other grants bodies had made it possible for the finest in Canadian and international talent to crisscross the country. Antal Dorati had conducted the Minneapolis Symphony on the ice surface of the old arena, Overture Concerts had brought Byron Janis and Lois Marshall to the auditorium at Knox Church, Brandon College struggled with the inadequacies of "The Chapel", and the glorious opera house at old city hall was by now condemned.

Planning for a new civic auditorium, intended to celebrate Brandon's 75th anniversary in 1957, began at a meeting of city council on February 15, 1953. On October 3, 1962, Premier Duff Roblin authorized the building of an auditorium as a 1967 Centennial project. Financial shortfalls postponed the project several times, but the Western Manitoba Centennial Auditorium finally opened its doors officially to the public on Wednesday, October 1, 1969 in the midst of a week which featured performances by such groups as the Royal Winnipeg Ballet, the Western Manitoba Philharmonic Choir, the Singing Nun, Sister Rita Patenaude, and Wilf Carter and Kitty Wells. Initial fears that the building would prove a white elephant have been confounded, at least in part by the able management of Buck Matiowsky, Bill Farrer, and Lori Murray, and the expert technical direction of Peter Pochynok.

In August of 1968, Charles R. Bronfman, President of the House of Seagram and a member of a family with roots in Brandon, announced the donation of "The Explorer", the sculpture by Hungarian-born Victor Tolgesy which had been part of the sculpture garden at "Man and His World", better known as Expo 67. The piece is meant to symbolize the third dimension, referring not only to spatial exploration, but both lunar and sculptural exploration as well.

St. Matthew's Church is one of over thirty churches in Manitoba designed by Brandon architect W. A. Elliott. It has been described as one of the finest examples of Gothic architecture in Canada. The actual construction, started in 1912, was done by Wm. Bell.

St. Matthew's Cathedral and First Presbyterian Church are two Brandon churches which contain extensive collections of fine stained glass memorial windows. The great Centennial window, at the west end of First Presbyterian, was dedicated in 1967 in memory of the men and women who opened up the prairies.

Included in the window are representations of the early family, the log shelters, the first chuch in the Brandon Hills begun by the Rev. George Roddick, the North West Mounted Police, an itinerant preacher, harvesting activities, steam locomotives, the buffalo and the plains Indians, and the Coats of Arms of both Manitoba and Canada.

The first Anglican churches in Brandon carried on the old-country tradition of all-male choirs. The 1903 choir of St. Matthew's Church is shown standing behind the Rev. C. Harrington (left), and Rev. McAdam Harding, and conductor G. B. Coleman.

Church-sponsored youth groups have played an important role in the cultural history of Brandon. CGIT groups presented Vesper Services, Cubs and Scouts presented highly entertaining winter "stampedes" in the arena, young people's groups presented annual variety concerts featuring such well-known Brandon artists as Eric and Humphrey Davies, Mae Selwood, and Muriel (Bain) Guild.

With their pastor, Rev. Eaton, and their Sunday School superintendent, James Wade, three such groups are shown in First Baptist Church in the early Thirties: CGIT, Cubs, and Scouts.

The laying of the cornerstone for the Brandon Methodist Church, which would become known as First Methodist in 1910 when Victoria Avenue Methodist opened, and as First United in 1925 after church union, took place on May 5, 1899. Lady Arma Sifton laid the stone and a future lieutenant-governor, J. A. M. Aitkens, preached the sermon. People of all denominations, many of whom had withdrawn their own services for the day, joined with hundreds of Methodists to celebrate the first step in the building of the edifice which would be dedicated on November 5 of the same year. With the amalgamation of the congregations of First Church, St. Paul's, and Kemnay United in 1971, the building was demolished, eventually to be replaced by Lawson House senior citizens' home.

The cornerstone photograph also shows clearly Brandon's splendid city hall and opera house, a building which would likewise survive into the early Seventies.

The Winnipeg Free Press of Monday, March 28, 1932 carried a front-page story occupying two full-length columns in which W. E. Ingersoll described the dedication on the previous morning, Easter Sunday, of the Arma Sifton Carillon, presented by the four sons of Sir Clifford and Lady Sifton in memory of their mother. "Alcoves and galleries of the First United Church were filled to overflowing long before the dedication service began. Microphone connection had been made with St. Paul's church across the street and the late comers were afforded an opportunity to follow the service from that auditorium."

Authentic carillon were, and still are, rare in Western Canada, and the pealing of the fourteen bronze bells became a distinguishing feature of Brandon. Immediate neighbours protested the pealing of every quarter-hour, and very shortly only the hours were marked.

With the merging of the congregations of First United and St. Paul's into Central United, and the demolition of the original Methodist Church, the Sifton bells were put into temporary storage; the tower of St. Paul's was not structurally capable of housing the carillon. With the consent of the Sifton family, the carillon was donated to the International Peace Garden, where it is currently housed in a temporary tower awaiting the building of the new peace tower. The accompanying photograph shows Byron Doak and Mary (Henderson) Smart during the ceremony at which the bells were presented to the Peace Garden Board. Mrs. Smart had played the carillon from the day of its dedication until its dismantling in 1968, often in weather so cold that the steel cables and compressed air mechanism by which the bells were tolled would snap.

When Brandon citizens go to their places of worship, they make their communications with the Almighty in many forms. One of the newest faiths, and perhaps the smallest of the congregations, is Baha'i. This Spiritual Assembly of Baha'is in Brandon was elected in 1971. Baha'is all over the world elect their assembly of nine on April 21, which is celebrated as the day Baha'u'llah declared his mission. Baha'is believe in one God and they work toward the unity of mankind.

Holding the Symbol of the Greatest Name is Dr. J. Aidun with Mrs. Aidun at his right. Seated left and right of them are Mansur Derekhshan and Mrs. J. Brown respectively. In the front row are Mrs. D. Hurl, Roy Hurl, Dr. William Guy, Mrs. M. Guy, and John Dunn II.

Brandon can boast of a distinguished line of major choral ensembles, including the Brandon Choral Association shown in First Methodist Church during their performance of *Messiah* in 1914. The organ pipes shown behind the choir were rather rare in that they actually sounded the lower notes, as well as providing a decorative screen for lesser pipes.

Brandon's earliest choral society was Col. Francis J. Clark's Brandon Operatic Society which mounted elaborate productions during the 1890's. The most recent was the Western Manitoba Philharmonic Choir, organized by a committee headed by Chris Verhoef in May of 1965, and conducted first by Lucien Needham and later by Leonard Mayoh.

Revival meetings, often with leading evangelists from throughout the United States and Canada, and ecumenical prayer services provided considerable interest for early Brandonites. This particular service was being held in St. Paul's Presbyterian Church, the most commodious building in the city at that time. The photograph shows the original choir loft of what is now Central United Church.

A Christmas institution popular in many American cities was introduced to Brandon audiences in 1975 by Janine MacDonald, conductor of the Calvary Temple choir. The singing Christmas Tree was 25 feet high and accommodated some 28 choristers in its lighted branches. Performances were given to standing room audiences for three evenings each December from 1975 through 1979. Participants in the initial presentation included Eleanor Neufeld and Marion Piniuta (lower left).

138

The Christmas season, in Brandon as in so many surrounding rural communities, saw the greatest concentration of local cultural events: schools presented their Christmas concerts, every Sunday School mounted an ambitious pageant, church choirs spent long hours preparing special Christmas music — even so small a congregation as St. Andrew's Presbyterian gave annual readings of Handel's *Messiah*. Over the years, however, two Christmas events which had special popularity were the Schubert Choir concert — sometimes a superbly acted production fo Dickens' *A Christmas Carol* — and the Rotary Carol Festival. Begun in the 1950's, the Carol Festival eventually fell victim to its own popularity. St. Paul's United Church would be filled to standing room night after night as church choirs, junior choirs, school choirs, and community choirs performed individually and then joined the audience in mass singing.

The Rotary Carol Festival, like its predecessor, the Advent recitals given over CKX radio by school choirs conducted by Dilys Davies, introduced new music to Brandon audiences used to the traditional carols. One of the participants in the 1959 Carol Festival was the Brandon College Glee Club conducted by David Wilson.

With excellent acoustics, central location, and seating capacities approaching 2,000, Brandon's several downtown churches were much favoured by both local and visiting musical and literary groups. First Methodist Church, later First Church United, played host to such illustrious speakers as Nellie McClung, Edna Jacques, and Ernest Seton Thompson; to such notable soloists as Gladys Swarthout and Harry Lauder; and to such popular annual Brandon events as the music festival, college concerts, visits by the Winnipeg Schools Orchestra, and the annual concert by the Brandon Male Voice Choir, directed by John Davies.

The choir is pictured at their 1935 presentation of *The Desert* by Tomas. Principals for this performance were, L to R: Rev. McKinney, rector of St. Mary's Anglican Church as narrator; Shirley (Drysdale) Dilley, pianist; Dr. E. S. Bolton, bass soloist; Ruth Morgan, soprano soloist; John Davies, conductor; Mary (Henderson) Smart, organist; and Linton Kent of Winnipeg, tenor soloist.

Winnipeg has long held the distinction of producing the finest choral music in Canada, but Brandon also has a long and worthy choral tradition, especially in its schools. Such music supervisors as Dilys Davies, Alan Rumbelow, Ted Forrest, and Derek Morphy have inspired countless local teachers to prepare choirs for music festival appearances. The photograph shows the Earl Haig Choir of 1931. The Harrison High Chorale conducted by David Wilson, the Vincent Massey Girls' Choir directed by Tom Inglis, and the Neelin Choirs led by Derek Morphy have contributed much to Brandon's cultural enrichment over the past several decades. Earl Oxford was noted for its operettas in the Fifties; Meadows and George Fitton are only two of the school choirs which are presenting ambitious annual programs as we enter the Eighties.

The band and orchestral program which now flourishes in Brandon schools dates back to the early Sixties when Stan Turner conducted the Brandon Lions' High School Band. Successive conductors have included Dwayne Hendricks, Ann Sherbondy, Malcolm Ashby, and Daphne Marshall. The late Sam Harris is shown with one of the junior ensembles he conducted in the late Seventies.

In the pre-television years, Brandon supported a lengthy and varied season of dramatic productions, including *Prize Pigs*, the hit of 1940. Many of you will be able to identify those in the photograph from the cast list: Grenville Bates, Ruth Bland, Norine Burnett, Ella Cross, Mary Defoe, Jean Frazer, Maria Goldberg, Betty Guthrie, Gretta Hopeland, Bill Johnson, Margaret Lewis, Ruth McInnis, Murray MacPherson, Ann Murphy, Betty Schenen, Ken Stone, Dave Thomas.

Brandon schools have always been noted for the variety of musical and dramatic activities undertaken in individual schools. The Green Acres School orchestra is shown being conducted by Robert Coates during a concert in May, 1966.

During the 1930's, the students and staff of Brandon Collegiate Institute staged a series of musical comedies, complete with orchestral accompaniment. Productions were directed by Miss Clendenning, with the orchestra trained and conducted by Mr. Heselgrave, a prominent local musician who donated his time to the school.

This photograph shows the cast of *Crocodile Island*, presented on stage in the Collegiate Institute in March, 1932. The elaborate sets included real palm trees.

The lower photograph shows the cast of a later production, *She Stoops to Conquer*.

There were eight teachers on the staff of Earl Oxford Junior High in 1951-52, making the school's full-fledged production of Humperdinck's famous opera, *Hansel and Gretel*, a particularly ambitious undertaking. Performances were given to standing-room audiences at City Hall on December 18 and 19. Music supervisor Dilys Davies and art supervisor Betty McLeish assisted Muriel Bowen and Edith Ward in directing the show which featured budding performances by such well-known Brandonites as Clair Davies, Karen (Constable) McKenzie, Jean (Wilkie) Brown, Joyce (Hart) Lumbard, Karen (Coates) Barteaux, and David Wilson.

The first of the contemporary Broadway musicals presented by a Brandon high school was *My Fair Lady*, directed for Harrison High School by David C. Wilson. The elaborate costumes for the February, 1965 production were created by Marjorie Fitton and the sets were executed by Mary Hume. Later shows mounted by the same team included *Oliver!*, *Camelot*, and *West Side Story*.

Leads were, L to R: Janet McPherson, Jack Woodward as Higgens, Jennifer (Campbell) Tegg as Eliza, Dale Brawn as Col. Pickering, and Gerrie Campbell.

Vincent Massey High School has also presented a number of musicals, both Broadway shows and original scripts, directed by Tom Inglis, Margaret Lysenko, Rudy Krahn, and in recent years, David C. Wilson.

The cast of *Oliver!* included, L to R: Karen Croker as Nancy, Geoff Hicks as the Artful Dodger, David Robertson as Oliver Twist, Brian Cottom as Fagin, and Pat (Stephenson) Cottom as Bet. The production was seen by over 4,200 people during five shows at the Western Manitoba Centennial Auditorium in April, 1976.

Brandon was one of the first communities in Canada to get its own radio station, as demonstrated by the three call letters of CKX, rare among privately-owned stations. The community was served well by its radio station, which presented a wide variety of local programming, including a number of shows featuring Brandon College talent. With the advent of television in the mid-Fifties, local programming took on the heightened appeal of visual impact.

One of the most successful and lasting of the local programs has been the quiz show for high school students, "Reach for the Top". In 1967, the Western Manitoba division of twenty-one schools was won by a quartet from Harrison High School, L to R: Bob Horobin, Larry Reynolds, Bob Smith (seated), and Don Skogstad. The team was coached by Jim Skinner.

Organized in 1927 by a British war bride, Mrs. Malcolm McGregor, the Brandon Little Theatre presented six seasons in the Normal School. After a lapse of several years, the group was re-organized by Marjorie McKenzie, moved to the city hall auditorium, and reached a pinnacle of success with *A Room in the Tower*, the play which won the group an invitation to appear in the Dominion Drama Festival. Shown preparing for their performance at the festival in London, Ontario, the first week of May, 1947, are, L to R: Kathleen Thordarson, Doreen McGill and Gwen Secter.

Brandon Little Theatre gave way in the early Sixties to New World Theatre, organized by a group which included Sigrid Green and Terry Hudson. After several seasons of straight drama, including *Our Town, Ghosts,* and *Picnic,* New World switched to musical theatre, under the impetus of Don S. Williams, and performed *Oklahoma, Guys and Dolls,* and *South Pacific* to standing room crowds.

Additional theatre was produced by the Brandon College Dramatic Society, and from 1933 an unbroken string of drama has been staged by such directors as Marjorie McKenzie, Sigrid Green, Edith Laycock, Don Lequesne, Evan Pepper, and currently, by Cedric Vendyback.

Brandon audiences routinely fill the Westman Auditorium for performances by students of the Royal Winnipeg Ballet School as coached by Barbara Ehnes; earlier audiences thrilled to the students of Almena Yeomans as they performed their first steps: (L to R) Ella Rosenman, Sybil Park, M. Bourke, Margaret Thornton.

Long before the advent of the Royal Winnipeg Ballet gave rise to Brandon's strong contemporary interest in dance, such local choreographers as Almena Yeomans were producing original ballets. Here the cast of *Deep Sea Ballet* is assembled on the Normal School stage for a performance which featured Vera Roney, Bea Graham, and John Majcher.

Ask anyone resident in Brandon in the Forties and Fifties to name a cultural institution and the answer will almost certainly be "the Schubert choir!" In the late Twenties Dr. Stuart Schultz, superintendent of the Brandon Hospital for Mental Diseases and later Mayor of Brandon, organized a group of about twenty youngsters, some of whom were to form the nucleus of the Schubert Choir. These children, who sang and danced and gave dramatic readings and panto-mimes, were known as the Brandon Kiddies.

Returning home the day after presenting a concert in Baldur, Manitoba, they stopped at Riverside Park for a dip in the Souris River. Still, they must rehearse, so Dr. Schultz is conducting them in some water music.

From front to the end of the row, the "kiddies" are Jeanne McDowell, Allan King, Frances Howard, Edward Wood, Lillian Bain, Marie Barager, Joe Robertson, Kathleen King, Edna Clark, Bob Howe, Francis Bain.

Some 400 young people had gone through the ranks of the Kiddies' Choir when Dr. Schultz founded the Schubert Choir in 1938. For a number of years the choir consisted of girls only, but by 1949, when *The Gondoliers* was the production, boys and men had joined the ranks. Leads included, L to R, Joe Ross, Roberta (Wilkie) Rose, and Glen Milliken, who would himself direct some of the final musical productions of the choir.

Year after year for almost two decades, the city hall opera house would ring to the strains of Gilbert and Sullivan, Sigmund Romberg, and Victor Herbert, and night after night, full houses would applaud the lavish productions.

In April of 1974, former choir members returned to Brandon from across Canada and the United States to honour Dr. and Mrs. Schultz, shown seated in the centre of the front row of the reunion photograph taken in the ballroom of the Canadian Inn.

The 1958-59 season marked the inception in Brandon of an annual series of four concerts organized by Jeunesses Musicales du Canada, or JMC. The first Brandon recital was given by renowned French cellist, Guy Fallot, accompanied by Brandon's own Lorne Watson.

In the mid-Sixties it was customary to follow each recital with a reception either at the Allied Arts Centre or the foyer of the new Music Building at Brandon University, to provide students who were studying music at the School of Music with an opportunity to meet the guest artist.

Brandon College, and then Brandon University, have contributed immeasurably to the cultural growth of Brandon and area. In earlier years, recitals by faculty members were supplement by concerts given by touring artists brought to Brandon by the music department. In later years the College and University have sponsored an increasing number of recitalists of high calibre, often without admission charges to the public. The opening of the J. R. C. Evans Lecture Theatre in the fall of 1961 and the new music building in 1963 considerably expanded the possibilities for presenting a wider variety of attractions.

In recent memory, the School of Music has had only two directors: Dr. W. L. Wright, from 1927 to 1947, and Dr. Lorne Watson, retiring this fall, (1981).

A recital was given in First Church United, Brandon, on Tuesday, May 6, 1947, to mark Dr. Wright's retirement after a career which saw him graduate sixty students with the ATCM diploma. Music graduates from all parts of Canada and several U.S. states gathered for the concert presented by, L to R: Peggy Sharpe, Dr. W. L. Wright, Esther Moore, Kathleen Fairbairn, Matilda Dallas, Edith McKee, Adeline Evans, Mary Smart, and Shirley Dilley.

"Canada is a good country, but she is too young for music. The people — they do not know — in the old land it was different . . . go to the little towns and villages, the people need your music . . . don't let them forget the old and the beautiful. Play for the people and Gott bless you." So spoke an elderly German patient in the Sanatorium to Hester Elliott, with tears in his eyes after he heard the concert presented by the Elliott Family Orchestra back about 1921.

That is exactly what they did. The family of eight, under their mother's direction, gave concert after concert in small towns and cities of Western Canada and the United States until about 1927. They travelled in all kinds of weather, sometimes playing under almost unbearable conditions.

This photo shows the Elliotts' van at rest in a front of a sod-thatched cottage near Wroxton, Saskatchewan.

The opera house, with seating for 540, was the cultural centre of Brandon for some six decades. Shakespearean companies from England performed annually for the first fourteen years of the century, succeeded by local productions mounted by Madame Marjorie Johnson and the Brandon Light Opera Company, twelve years of such British musicals as *The Maid of the Mountains*. Later occupants of the opera house were the Schubert Choir and New World musicals, Brandon Little Theatre and Brandon College dramas, and a wide variety of touring attractions ranging from Gracie Fields to Roy Rogers and Trigger, who ascended to the stage via the three long flights of outdoor stairs on the west wall.

The city hall and opera house had been built by F. T. Cope, whose contract provided that he complete the building on or before January 1, 1892 or face a stiff penalty. A public school entertainment held in the opera house on Friday, December 22, 1893, cost 25 cents for adults and 15 cents for children.

The final curtain call for the Neelin High School production of Gilbert and Sullivan's operetta, "Ruddigore", did not move the figures in the framed portrait studies shown in the background of this photo. Do you remember that performance in March of 1970 when the figures represented in the frames actually *did* step out to become part of the production?

Directed by Derek Morphy, the cast included such people as Tricia Cantwell, Catherine Gross, Francesca Green, Margaret MacNaughton, Laurie Milliken, Terry McDougall, Ken Halsey, Jim Marshall, Ken De Roov, Allan Guest, and Kim Gemmill.

Without television to bring instant pictures of the latest fashions, and with few magazines able to afford the luxury of coloured illustrations, Brandon women in the Thirties and Forties depended on the many local fashion shows to keep them in touch with haute couture. Many of the shows were in aid of some local charity, such as the hospital.

Members of the Schubert Choir are shown on November 9, 1949, prior to a show in which they modelled furs from Yaeger's, hats from Lucette's, shoes from Creelman's, with make-up courtesy of Brown's Drug Store and hair styled by Scory's. Models are, back, L to R: Sheila (Schultz) Taylor, Kay (Henderson) Ross, Betty McCulloch, Alice Bunch, Elizabeth McGregor; front: Beth Paterson, Arden (Constable) Doig, Diane Taylor, Roberta (Wilkie) Rose.

Can you imagine the hours that have been spent preparing the elaborate dresses worn by these women at one of Brandon's earlier fairs? We do not have a date for this photo, but one description of the events at the Summer Fair in 1905 tells that the "...noble red men attended in all their gorgeousness, marched by the grandstand to the sound of tom toms". This marked the first year an Indian pow-wow was presented at the Fair.

This group of young women, organized for social and cultural self-improvement, still had fun dressing up for a tea in the Security Block. These members of Beta Sigma Phi — Delta chapter — circa 1945, assumed more serious careers than their gypsy costumes suggest.

Taking part in Brandon's 50th anniversary celebrations in 1932 was this group of Ukrainian dancers, wearing dress typical of that of the old Ukraine. From L to R, back row: Mark . . . , Steve Lestition, Stan Surby, Peter Cymbalist; front row: . . . Nazer, Polly Shadlack, Mary Rekis, Mary Michael.

Remember the old song about seeing Nellie home from Aunt Dinah's quilting party? Well, this is not Aunt Dinah's, but obviously the fellows attended those parties in 1900, and really took a hand in the quilting. This one took place in Brandon, and the former Miss Verda Wrye is the only one who can be identified, fourth from the left.

Besides quilting bees, people used to hold barn-raising bees. This day's work will end with a great supper and perhaps a dance as well. After that, "seeing Nellie home".

Here is one of the large crowds that attended the popular whist drive and dance functions at the Imperial Gardens. The inset shows Jack Jewsbury, who opened the Imperial in 1934.

During the war all Brandon's night spots were busy places: the Palladium on Rosser Avenue; the Esquire on Tenth, and in this photo, the Imperial at the corner of Tenth and Princess. People would line up in early evening waiting for the Imperial Gardens to open at 8:30.

One of the bands that played at the Imperial Dance Gardens during the mid-Thirties was The Olympians. The leader, Russ Isadore, came to Brandon from Winnipeg. He now resides in North Carolina.

One of the most popular dance bands that played at the Imperial Dance Gardens was Roy Brown and his Orchestra. They played Clear Lake during the latter Thirties and in winter played at the Esquire and the Imperial, but accepted other engagements as well. In this photo, they are about to leave Clear Lake for the 1940 Labour Day weekend dance at The Cave, one of Winnipeg's sophisticated night spots during the late Thirties and the Forties.

The band had the distinction of being the only Canadian dance band with five brothers: Frank, Tom, Joe, Percy and Roy Brown (front). The other musicians were: Vic Gelbert, Bob McCulloch, Jay Hannay, Del Davies, Al La Fontaine, Sig Johnson. Their rise to popularity, according to one newspaper report, was said to have been "nothing short of phenomenal."

Among the first of the European immigrants in Brandon were the Polish. In 1913 they organized the Polish Sokol Association, and in this photo taken in 1938 they are celebrating their 25th anniversary.

Brandonites of other backgrounds have found that a good social time is to be had when they attend a function at the Sokol Hall.

154

About 1916 the Ukrainian immigrants in Brandon built a hall at 1133 Stickney Avenue which they named The Ukrainian National Home. Their purpose was to preserve their language and their culture, and to pass this heritage on to their children. They formed a drama club which provided both entertainment and a learning experience.

This picture is that of the original front-stage drop curtain done in oils and used for hundreds of productions. Now framed and strengthened to preserve it, it is a wall-hanging in the new National Home built in 1969 on the same site.

The scene depicts a village in the Ukraine. It kept memories of the homeland alive for the pioneers. Scenes similar to this can be found on stages in many of the Ukrainian halls across our country.

" . . . I couldn't resist the urge to revisit the scene of so many class picnics and so drove to Lake Clementi. I must confess it seemed smaller and less romantic than then . . . . The fortunate few [girls] who were taken boating — not every boy could finance the treat at 25¢ per hour — had a conversation piece to last till term end . . . . [We] wished we were old enough to stay and dance in the pavilion," writes a former BCI student recalling her life in Brandon.

"I'll never forget how annoyed I used to feel when Eastern boys laughed at our slough. To me it was a lovely spot. Picnics were picnics in those days — such food! veal and ham pies, roasts, hot scalloped potatoes, cakes and fruit," recalled another former Brandonite, Hilda Hesson.

The development of a resort area at Clear Lake in 1927 brought a gradual end to outings at Lake Clementi.

Not many families in Brandon had a summer place in 1913. The enterprising boys in the W. A. Elliott family saved up their earnings from paper routes and helped to buy a small piece of land just south of Richmond about 3rd Street. Here the family spent their summer holidays away from their city home on Seventh Street. When your father is a leading architect in your home city, you can expect to have a well-built summer cottage.

The entire Elliott family posed for this picture.

"One generation passeth away and another generation cometh . . . " is part of the inscription on the cairn erected at Kirkham's Bridge by the Women's Institute in 1970 to commemorate Manitoba's centenary. This snapshot, taken under Kirkham's Bridge in 1939, shows two generations of the Campbell family and some friends. Top: Jim Campbell, Bob Imlach. Centre: Doreen Campbell and friend. Front: Bill Campbell, Maurice Campbell, Jim Imlach, Annie and Bill Calder.

Kirkham's Bridge, still a popular picnic spot, was first built in 1895 and washed out in 1897. An iron bridge built in 1906 served until quite recently when a third bridge was constructed.

Over the years Brandon

residents have pitched their tents here for their summer vacations; Boy Scouts have camped here; artists have found the bridge a subject for their paintings.

Many Brandon youngsters have an opportunity to attend camps during the summer — camps sponsored by churches and community organizations. These two kids are waiting patiently for their ride which will take them to a camp at Clear Lake, sponsored by the Children's Aid Society and paid for in a large part by the Brandon Rotary Club.

Attending Y camp introduces these lads to unforgettable experiences. Don Snyder, the fourth from the left, and Charles McNaughton at the far right, are the only two we can name. The year? Perhaps 1924. Boys' bathing suits at that time had tops, so the suits must have been hanging on tree branches to dry.

During the eartly Thirties, the Assiniboine River at the foot of Sixteenth Street provided a popular bathing beach. Three concessions operated all summer long, and gas lights made night-time swimming a special kind of recreation.

Early in the century Alderman J. B. Curran had envisioned a recreational park for our city. In 1921 land was acquired under a 99-year lease from the Department of Indian Affairs, but it was not until the 1960's that this popular swimming place became a reality.

157

# VIII   A Sporting City

Ever since the days when the first lacrosse players lined up their teams for practice sessions on Sixth Street, Brandon has steadily but surely built a reputation as a Sporting City. The city has nurtured countless athletes who have achieved widespread attention, particularly in the field of hockey. Citizens of Brandon and the surrounding area have shown their support of sports to the extent that the city was chosen to host the Canada Winter Games in 1979. Brandon's inheritance from this event includes, among other things, some of the finest sports facilities in the country.

Following are but a few photographs which may help to recall some of the sporting events that Brandonites have enjoyed in the past.

The official opening of the Keystone Centre is the occasion of this assembly, April 2, 1973. James Richardson, Minister of Supply and Services, is delivering one of the addresses. From L to R, from the unidentified RCMP officer, are: Doug Lawson; Eugene Whelan, Minister of Agriculture; Len Evans, Minister of Industry and Commerce; Mayor W. K. Wilton; Mrs. McKeag; Lt.-Gov. W. J. McKeag; Governor-General Roland Mitchener, who officially opened the Centre; Mrs. Mitchener; Fred McGuinness; James Moffatt, President of the Provincial Exhibition; Lt.-Col. W. Manson.

158

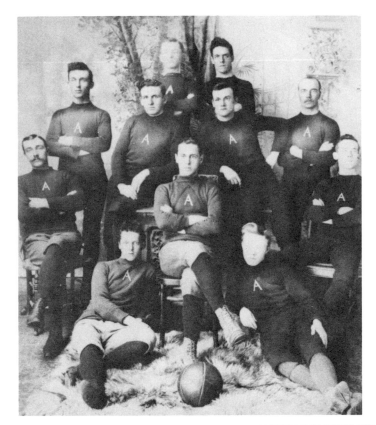

Soccer football was one of the sports included in the Brandon Academy's program back in 1890. Professor McKee was President of the club. Top, L to R: Jas. Smith, F. Wheeldon. Row 3: J. O. Gunn, Dickson, E. Gothard, E. Graham. Seated: J. W. Curry, J. B. Cain, J. Keeler. Front; E. Bennest, M. D. Cavanagh.

Lacrosse was one game people took seriously back at the turn of the century. It was traditionally Canada's national game. Lacrosse derived from a game, *baggataway*, played by Indians in eastern Canada. The name *lacrosse* was the word used by the French to describe the hooked racquet-like stick.
City Council gave consent to the use of Sixth Street as a lacrosse pitch, 'way back.

The Canadian Lacrosse Association, founded in 1925, annually awards the Minto Cup to the Junior Championship team. This 1891 team would in all likelihood have been worthy contenders for such a trophy.

Some readers may find their forebears among the members of this team. Back row: W. Currie, Tom Lowes, Sandy Fleming, Bob Holden, Frank Wheeldon. Centre: Fred Knight, E. Chipperfield, Ed King, Sid Marland, Bob Brown. Front; Jas. Smith, Jas. Hamilton, Willie Blackwell.

Hockey was a relatively new game when this photo was taken in Brandon back in the 1880's. The game was invented about 1860, and the first rule book written in 1879.

The fellows here have just played a benefit game to raise funds to build a hospital in Brandon. It was married men vs. the single guys. Among the players we can identify a number: Front row, L to r: Bob Clark, Dr. Powers, mascot, Sheriff . . . (goal), Bert Sylvester, Bob Harper. Centre: Bert Sutherland, Peter Payne, Architect W. H. Shillinglaw, Bob Campbell, Ed Hanbury. Back: Murdoch McKenzie, A. J. Kirkcaldy, Gordon Hinley, George Mutter, Dr. J. S. Matheson, Sr., B. McKay.

That's *both* teams — fourteen players and their managers.

The 1938-39 season gave the Brandon Elks sufficient wins to play in the Western finals for the Abbott Cup. They lost to Edmonton — by a single goal, and had to be content with having won the Manitoba and Thunder Bay Regional Cup.

The players, lined up with their coach "Jimmy" Creighton, are J. Henry, Billy Klem, Glen Harmon, Herbie Burron, Glen Richardson, Chuck Taylor, Ray Neilson, Freddie Johnson, Cameron, "Buzz" Witcherley, Sandy Shear.

Many will recall the exciting 1959-60 hockey season when the Brandon Wheat Kings successfully came through the first lap to the Memorial Cup by winning the Manitoba and Thunder Bay Championship. They lost out to Edmonton, however, in the Western play-offs.

This 1978-79 Brandon Wheat Kings team gave its fans some of the best hockey they had seen in a long time. They had just finished a gruelling schedule of travel, playing 27 games in the play-off series. The Memorial Cup was within reach, but in a tight final game with a score of 1-1 at the end of the third period the delicate balance of overtime play tilted against them.

Back row, L to R: Dr. Trevor Lawrence, team physician; Larry Roberts; Don Dietrich; Steve Patrick; Don Gillen; Brad Kempthorne; Dave McDowell; Kelly Elcombe; Jack Stouffer, trainer. Centre row: Art Marshall, honourary trainer; Wes Coulson; Brant Kiessig; Brian Propp; Kelly McCrimmon; Dave Stewart; Dave Chartier; Darren Gusdal; Laurie Boschman. Front row: Rick Knickle; Ray Allison; Dunc McCallum, coach; Brad McCrimmon; Jack Brockest, general manager; Tim Lockridge; Scott Olson.

The sign in the background may have significantly encouraged someone to get this team organized. Let this picture be worth the proverbial thousand words, for enquire as we may we could not come up with anyone who could tell us who? when? or even how? or why? But it *is* the Brandon Wheat King sweaters they are wearing.

Ladies did play hockey back in 1898 or thereabouts when this photo was taken. Only one name is visible identifying, presumably, the owner of the hockey stick: M. E. Cottingham.

Youngsters today are fully-equipped to play hockey after the patterns set by the "Wheaties" and other favourite teams in the National League. Televised games supplement the coaching given at the neighbourhood rinks. Bradley Milne and Darren Sutherland have started their hockey careers well decked out — like the pro's.

Playing hockey when Brandon's "Turk" Broda was a kid was fairly basic. You played on the Assiniboine River, or on an open air rink which you helped to flood. And if you aspired to be a goalie like Turk, you padded yourself with Eaton's and Simpson's catalogues, and invited the kids to shoot pucks at you.

This is part of the early background that helped shape Turk Broda into one of the finest goaltenders the sports world has ever known.

Turk played a season with the Brandon Native Sons in 1932-3, the next year with the Winnipeg Monarchs, and then with the Detroit Red Wings' farm team when Conn Smythe spotted him and signed him up with the Toronto Maple Leafs. He was with the Leafs from 1936 - 51 except for a three-year stint with the Canadian Army.

When he retired from the Leafs in 1951 his two brothers joined him in a toast to the Stanley Cup. Turk is at the left; Lou, foreman at the Gardens, is at centre; and Stan, ar right, was ice maker at the Gardens.

Baseball was first introduced to Brandon about 1885 and then the game was played more as "a gas" than as the serious game it is today. For example, one team played on roller skates against another team who would have to use bicycles to get from base to base. On one occasion in 1885, the lawyers and bankers (and there were lots of those in Brandon that year) played against the All-comers. The professionals won 197 to 180. All rulings were made from the lacrosse manual! Baseball rules were probably on the way. The mail was slow then.

But the Brandon Greys, as the photo suggests, had achieved a more professional-like status by 1921. These fellows look as if they would take the game more seriously.

The Maple Leaf Baseball Club came out winners of the intermediate league in Manitoba back in 1908. There are some familiar names among them: Back row, L to R: C. Mummery, J. Ball, P. Paterson (manager), J. Doughty (pitcher), A. Reid. Centre: L. Haywood, E. Lewis (catcher), H. Curtis (pitcher), J. McNeill. Front: C. Crane, B. Crane (mascot), J. Pope.

Back in 1924, three city teams, The Tigers, The Maroons, and The Bearcats, gave their fans lots of opportunities to see good baseball. At the end of that season, the Brandon Maroons, representing the central city area, gained top position. From L to R the players are, top: Joe McIntosh, Bobby Crane, Wally Brannan, Hode Cowan; centre: Frank Winteringham, President H. A. McNeill, Manager D. F. Winteringham, John Plum; bottom: Tommy Cowan, Jimmy Hughes, Johnny Rogers, Frank Johnson, Hap Buchanan.

Yes, they really did play tennis in those dresses back in 1900. Henry Badger is the chap in the foreground about to serve.

Brandon's first tennis court was on the southeast corner of Fourteenth and Louise. The bare horizon can only emphasize how the city has developed.

While we do see people on the courts in the city today, the sport does not appear to have achieved the prominence held by other summer sports.

The Tennis Club Tea was one of *the* social functions of the summer in Brandon at the turn of the century. This is the 1906 tea.

It was 1884 when the first game of curling was played in Brandon. On January 16 the Captain Wastie rink played Judge D. M. Walker. They finished the last end by lamplight.

This rink won the Lieutenant-Governor's Trophy at the Winnipeg Bonspiel in 1898. From L to R they are: G. H. Smith, Wm. Henderson, Jno. Inglis, W. L. Parrish.

Hockey has to be put on the back burners when a bonspiel is scheduled in any town. Here are some hockey referees who were put on low simmer when they lost out to these curling hotshots in a Brandon Bonspiel about 1966. This eight-ender, played by Don Gamble's Brandon rink, didn't need a referee to declare it, only to believe it.

The Gamble rink included Angus McLeod as skip, Ed Bauldic, and Lloyd McDonald. The referees include the then *Sun* sportswriter, Laurie Artiss, Monty Montgomery, and Ken Fowles, with Jack Caldwell of Hamiota skipping.

Your guess is as good as ours as to who is throwing the rock in the inset.

Cross-country skiing was unheard of back in 1936 when this snap was taken. You snowshoed or skied downhill — no happy medium.

MacArthur's offered special excursion rates to the dam (now called Glenorky) for 25 cents return. On this trip, however, the skiers had started out for Winnipeg to catch the ski special to La Riviere. Unfortunately, the bus froze up, so they never did get that weekend of skiing.

Sleighing near the Assiniboine has assumed a more sophisticated mode in this 1974 photo. Skidooing in tandem makes an exciting Sunday afternoon's excursion with the family.

These fellows are about to take another run on Sykes' Slide on a winter's day in 1927. Located on the south bank of the river near 33rd Street, the slide offered recreation to more than one generation of Brandon youngsters. Schools arranged for at least one toboggan party a year for their classes, but obviously the use of the slide was enjoyed by other than school kids. We can name G. Baldock at the left. Don Graham, head waiter at the Prince "Eddy", is the chap in front.

Ice fishing on the Assiniboine is another sport popular with Brandon families. This photo of an outing of two families was taken in 1974.

168

Seeing a display like this reminds one of the old cigarette ad — "so round, so firm, so fully packed". Dr. Wilfred Bigelow, Sr. and his son Bill have had a good mallard shoot. This photo was taken in 1924 when there was no limit on a day's bag.

Dr. Bigelow, one of Brandon's pioneer doctors, came west as a young man from Nova Scotia in 1898. He established the first medical clinic in Canada in the Clement Block in 1913. Associated with him in those first years were Drs. H. S. Sharpe and L. J. Carter. By 1918 he was joined by Drs. R. O. McDiarmid. S. J. Pierce, and R. P. Cromarty. Miss Jean

McDonald was the Bigelow Clinic's first lab technician.

A skilled surgeon, Dr. Bigelow also wrote with dry humour of some of his early medical cases as well as his hunting and fishing experiences.

Sons Bill, an eminent heart surgeon, and Dan, an orthopedic surgeon, live in Toronto and Winnipeg respectively.

In October 1882 an early settler, William Lothian, wrote his brother in Scotland advising him to be sure to bring a good gun when he came to Canada.

"You'll get lots of duck shooting, also geese," he wrote. "You may have the satisfaction of bringing down a deer or a moose. Farther west the buffalo may afford you an exciting hunt. Thousands of them have been killed this winter and are reported numerous 150 miles west of Brandon. And to think you were brought before a magistrate for killing a paltry rabbit! Alas, poor Scotland . . . ."

Some 45 years later two of Brandon's prominent sportsmen bagged this six-point elk in the Riding Mountains. It dresses at nearly 600 pounds, giving Dr. Charles Powers (L) and Dave Clement a good portion of their winter's meat supply in 1927.

This is sport of a kind for the boys and the spectators at the Winter Fair, but obviously not for the calf.

Here are some chaps from City Hall pulling together and apparently enjoying it, circa 1970. We don't know whom they are pulling against, however. Mayor Bill Wilton is up front, and Jack Brockest and Elwood Gorrie are giving a mighty good tug.

When firemen were not busy putting out fires in the early 1900's, they found time to sponsor the occasional cribbage tournament. The Loyal Orange Lodge took away the trophy from the 1909 event. Standing, from L to R: J. W. McFadden, Wm. Hurler, James Craig. Seated: Henry Koester, A. G. Smith, D. A. Sutherland, E. J. Hutchison.

*Jim Walsh by pumping station.*

Recreation takes many forms. If you are not keen on competitive sports, try this one. Jim Walsh appears quite at ease, with arms akimbo.

We are not sure this fellow got off the ground with his flying contraption. Our pioneer flyers have no recollection of this endeavour, but the camera doesn't lie.

*Jim Walsh by pumping station.*

Dress is optional for this sports event, held at the City Recreational Centre in the Seventies.

There was no concern about downtown traffic when Architect W. A. Elliott took the kids for an automobile ride up Rosser Avenue. He is driving a maroon-coloured Haynes-Opperson, circa 1905, obviously "with air".

Mr. Elliott is said to have been the first Brandonite to use his car for business travel. He is also credited with having organized the Brandon Auto Club.

As far back as 1906, these two Brandon women fearlessly took to driving on the open road. Miss Ford is at the wheel and her passenger is Miss Trotter. The vehicle probably belongs to the Fords. Driving the heavier automobile (a one-cylinder job) is T. B. Mitchell, with Harry Crowe and Jack Pritchard advising from the back seat. The license plates are 84 and 86, so there were at least that many automobiles in Manitoba that year.

In 1911 when this photo was taken there were about one hundred automobiles in Brandon. Editorially, the *Sun* commented on the number of people buying autos they could ill afford. The automobile was described as "this motor genie which somebody has let out of a bottle".

Brandon had its own automobile club, and here is one of the city's first car rallies lined up in front of the Empire Hotel, 725 Rosser Avenue, in 1911. The next year, in February, even though the temperatures had dipped to forty-three below, these enthusiasts took part in what they called the Victoria Avenue Driving Club matinee. One would suppose that was where "drag racing" got its start in Brandon. Local citizens objected to these matinees, understandably.

Brandon has been invaded! The silver cocoon-like vehicles are part of the Wally Byam cavalcade that visited the City in the mid-Seventies. The photo is a study of the precision of organization required to host such a visit, but does not portray the actual goodwill experienced during the occupation.

Tammy Josephson, a talented young Brandon figure skater, lights the flame to officially open the Canada Winter Games, February, 1979.

The Sportsplex was finished in time for the opening of the Canada Winter Games. None were more pleased than the Honourable Iona Campagnola, Minister of Fitne s and Amateur Sport, and Alex Matheson, President of the Winter Games Society.

There are too many things going on for the conductor to expect rapt attention. This is a small segment of the massed choir in attendance at the Games.

All athletes participating in the Canada Winter Games are assembled before the massive crowd that witnessed the thrilling opening ceremonies at Brandon's Keystone Centre.

# IX Happenings

In the life of any city, as in the lives of the people that make the city, there are occasions for celebration and occasions to mourn; there are moments to be cherished forever and moments to be recalled with regret. Many people have loaned photos which recall such events, and we present them here.

In our day the automobile has been said to be the background most frequently chosen when having a picture taken. (Just check your own albums!) In this photo, circa 1884, the "wheels" providing the background was — what else — the Assiniboine cart, parked in the spacious driveway.

It doesn't have to be an ox cart or a car that provides a background for a picture. Katherine Stinson dropped down at the Provincial Exhibition in 1916 so these Indians, in all their finery, posed for this picture with Miss Stinson. She took a side trip to Camp Hughes that same day.

It was reported that aviatrix Katherine Stinson "flipped her wings" in an unscheduled landing in a Douglas grainfield after she had visited the trenches "somewhere in Canada", in 1916.

Miss K. Stinson, Aviatrice,
In Military Trenches.
"Somewhere in Canada"—

"His patriotism was sincere. He was regarded as one of the best officers among the Canadian men." This was Major Joseph McLaren, one of Brandon's first losses in World War I.

Joseph McLaren came to Brandon from Dundee, Scotland as a young man. In 1904 he joined the Brandon teaching staff and served as physical education instructor for ten years. During this time he enlisted in the 12th Manitoba Dragoons and soon rose to the rank of Major. When war broke out he was among the first to go to the front.

These school cadets are learning some of the disciplines of war.

These recruits at Camp Hughes, ca. 1915, have a fair amount of training to endure before they will lead a parade. Camp Hughes was located somewhat east of the present Camp Shilo.

The First Depot Battalion, 650-strong, marches down Rosser Avenue in early June, 1918 to embark shortly for overseas service. The war ended only a few months later.

# Thanksgiving Celebration and Service

on the occasion of the

## Peace Declaration

BRANDON, MANITOBA

Monday, November 11th, 1918

Under the auspices of the City Council

COMMITTEE:
Mayor Cater; S. E. Clement, M.P.P.; Doctor Whidden, M.P.;
Rev. A. E. Smith; H. Brown,
Great War Veterans' Association in attendance.

*Addresses*

*by*

MAYOR CATER, CHAIRMAN

S. E. CLEMENT, M.P.P.

MAJOR WHILLIER

DOCTOR WHIDDEN, M.P.

N.B.—The speakers are kindly requested to occupy not more than five minutes.

### Public Religious Service

1. HYMN: "O God Our Help in Ages Past."

   O God, our help in ages past,
   Our hope for years to come,
   Our shelter from the stormy blast,
   And our eternal home.

   Beneath the shadow of Thy throne,
   Thy saints have dwelt secure;
   Sufficient is Thine arm alone,
   And our defence is sure.

   *TUNE—St. ANNE*
   Before the hills in order stood,
   Or earth received her frame,
   From everlasting Thou art God,
   To endless years the same.

   Time, like an ever-rolling stream
   Bears all its sons away;
   They fly forgotten, as a dream
   Dies at the opening day.

   O God, our help in ages past,
   Our hope for years to come,
   Be Thou our guide while life shall last,
   And our eternal home.   Amen.

2. ADDRESS: Rev. A. E. Smith, President Brandon Ministerial Association.

3. PRAYER: Rev. S. R. Hammond, Chaplain Great War Veterans' Association.

4. HYMN: "Lord of the Lands."

   *TUNE—O CANADA!*
   Lord of the lands, beneath Thy bending skies,
   On field and flood, where'er our banner flies,
   Thy people lift their hearts to Thee,
   Their grateful voices raise;
   May our Dominion ever be
   A temple to Thy praise.
   Thy will alone let all enthrone;
   Lord of the lands, make Canada Thine own!   (Repeat).

   Almighty Love, by Thy mysterious power,
   In wisdom guide, with faith and freedom dower;
   Be ours a nation evermore
   That no oppression blights,
   Where justice rules from shore to shore,
   From lakes to Northern lights.
   May love alone for wrong atone;
   Lord of the lands make Canada Thine own. (Repeat).

   Lord of the worlds, with strong eternal hand,
   Hold us in honor, truth, and self-command;
   The loyal heart, the constant mind,
   The courage to be true,
   Our wide-extending Empire bind,
   And all the earth renew.
   Thy name be known through every zone;
   Lord of the worlds, make all the lands Thine own.   (Repeat).   Amen.

   The combined Bands of the 99th Regiment and the Salvation Army will lead the musical features of the service.

   Mr. H. Brown will direct the singing.

5. GOD SAVE THE KING.

*Dawn*

You that have faith to look with fearless eyes
Beyond the tragedy of a world at strife,
And trust that out of night and death shall rise
The dawn of ampler life:

Rejoice, whatever anguish rend your heart,
That God has given you for a priceless dower,
To live in these great times and have your part
In Freedom's crowning hour.

That you may tell your sons who see the light
High in the heavens, their heritage to take—
"I saw the powers of darkness put to flight!
I saw the morning break!"

—*Sir Owen Seaman*

Armistice Day, 1918 was celebrated with a parade through Brandon streets and a service of thanksgiving.

The Cumming family float expresses some of the joy felt by Brandon families that the war was finally over. The lad standing at attention is Gordon Cumming, with his aunts and uncles seated around the hearth.

179

Bill Sutherland, shown here with his wife and daughter and some other youngsters, entered this float in the Armistice Day parade celebrating the end of World War I.

Remembrance is a solemn occasion, as shown on the faces of these women and children who are about to place flowers in memory of loved ones.

The day after the fire these inmates are making their way through Brandon to the old Wheat City Arena. There they were to spend two years before they could be relocated elsewhere. They are shown crossing over the First Street bridge and past the Empire Brewing Plant. The shell of the Asylum building is barely perceptible on the horizon.

Brandon had, in the early days, more than its share of devastating fires. This skeleton of a building was the Insane Asylum, located on the hill northeast of the city. Fire broke out there on November 4, 1910. Six hundred and forty-three patients had been evacuated to spend the rest of the night in other buildings on the grounds.

A fire can always draw a crowd. The blaze here is in the Telephone Exchange at 31 Ninth Street, July 24, 1913. It seems to have drawn an all-male group of spectators, save for the lady in white.

This photo was taken near Treherne, Manitoba in 1906. After the blizzard in mid-January, 1916, a train pulling into Brandon might well have looked like this one.

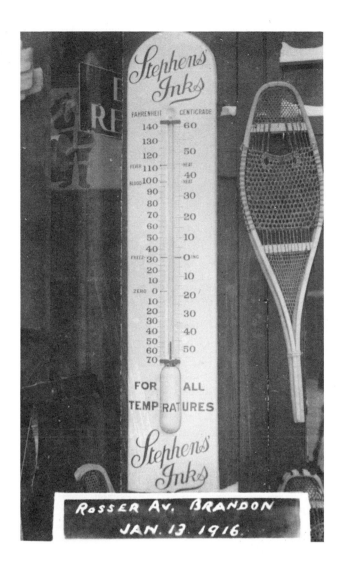

ROSSER AV. BRANDON
JAN. 13. 1916.

Any way you read this thermometer, Centigrade or Fahrenheit, it was mighty cold in Brandon on January 13, 1916. A raging blizzard had dumped six feet of snow on the city, and hundreds of men had been called to shovel out the CPR yards.

The men loaded the snow onto a flatcar train which took the load to the bridge. Here the snow was shovelled into the river. Train No. 3 was due so the snowtrain was run onto a lead line in the yards to wait until the main line was clear. The crew went into a caboose at the end of the snowtrain to warm up while waiting for No. 3. Someone neglected to close the switch. Number 3 finally arrived, and because visibility was zero due to whirling snow and steam, and because the switch was open to the lead line, the train plowed into the snowtrain. The flatcars became a deadly ramrod striking against the caboose in which about thirty workers were having their cup of tea. Seventeen men were killed. One man, who lived near the yards, had gone home for tea. When he learned of the disaster he returned home, took off his boots, and never again went back to work in the yards.

Four days after the disaster in the CPR yards, fire broke out in the Syndicate Block at the corner of Seventh Street and Rosser Avenue, where Eaton's stands today. The bitter cold had frozen the hydrants, making it impossible to control the fire. Four employees of Doig, Rankin and Robertson perished in the blaze. One of the survivors recalls that she leaped from an upper storey window, landing on the fire chief. They fell back into the deep snow and were saved from serious injury.

This photo was taken by Leslie Skinner, a young farmer from Alexander who happened to be in Brandon that day. On learning about the fire, he bought a camera and took this picture.

It was breakfast time for the Royal North West Mounted Police when this fire broke out in their horse barns, October 29, 1920. The men were barracked in the Armouries at Eleventh and Victoria with their horses housed in the "old" Winter Fair Building across the street. Despite heroic efforts to rescue the horses, thirty-one perished. Two men were injured trying to evacuate the animals which, because they were frightened by the crackling flames and the smoke, fought off efforts to remove them.

The Winter Fair building had been built in 1907 and it was here that Brandon's first Winter Fair was held in 1908. As well, it served as a concert auditorium, and from 1914 to 1916 it was used as one of Canada's alien detention centres.

This photo of Constable Larkins on his horse was taken before the fire. To save his mount, Constable Larkins wound the reins around his wrist to pull the horse out through the smoke. Near the entrance a heavy fireball came down from the roof and struck the animal and then Larkins, knocking him out. The horse, though badly burned, continued out of the building, dragging his own rescuer to safety. Unhappily, the horse was so badly burned it had to be shot.

This is Rosie, mascot of the RNWMP detachment during its brief stay in Brandon. Rosie was also at the barracks on that fateful morning of October 29. She had left her two pups in the horse barn while she went to have her breakfast. When the fire broke out she raced back and carried out her own rescue exercise, bringing out both pups in one trip.

Resembling freshly-washed fleeces hanging on a line to dry, the icicles here tell another grim story of a disastrous fire, this one on the west side of Tenth Street just north of the Strathcona Block. This time it was the Bowling Alley, the Stone Bakery, and a shoe store. The date — February 3, 1932.

The Olympia Cafe fire of April 6, 1953 took the life of Fireman Frederick Brown during his attempt to rescue one of the tenants. Formerly the Bank of British North America, built in 1883, the Olympia was one of the more popular dining spots in the city.

Hundreds of spectators quickly gathered to watch the blaze, creating considerable problems for the police and the firemen.

It was after the this fire that City Council was called upon to examine the efficiency of both the Fire Department and the equipment.

The Assiniboine has flooded its basin numerous times in the past hundred or so years. One such "accident of nature" precipitated the change of intention by the Canadian Pacific Railway to establish a divisional point on the higher land on the south side of the river rather than at Grand Valley. Hopes for a great city to rise at the latter point were washed away by the flooding in 1881. This photograph shows the Assiniboine in flood in May, 1947. The houses are in the vicinity of 18th Street off McGregor Avenue.

Sitting pensively in her starched uniform is the first graduate of Brandon Hospital to receive a Registered Nurse certificate, Anna Catherine McLaren Kenner, lone graduate of the 1898 class. Nurse Kenner died in 1965 at the age of ninety-three.

Senior members of the nursing staff appear to be in consultation about how best to deal with this recalcitrant young lady, Miss Dell Cannon. Miss Christina McLeod, Superintendent of Nurses, is shown with Mrs. Hatcher and a sister of Miss Cannon.

This auspicious occasion is the laying of the cornerstone of the new General Hospital, July 18, 1921. Premier T. C. Norris, seated behind the table, performed the official act. Other distinguished attendees included Mr. D. McEwen, standing just left of centre; Miss Birtles, wearing a black dress and hat; Mayor George Dinsdale, standing hatless at right centre.

The Brandon General Hospital story is one of building and rebuilding; but it is also the story of service given by countless individuals. Among the nurses who have served the Hospital is this group which includes, at the left, Miss Ellen Birtles, who became Superintendent of Nurses in 1898. When she retired in August of 1919, among the many gifts presented her were a purse of gold and a travelling case lined with hundred dollar bills. Her associates in this 1929 photo are Mrs. Miller (nee Kettles), Miss Kettles, Miss Frances Birtles, Miss Dell Cannon.

What did nurses-in-training do in their free time in the late Thirties? For some weeks before this photo was taken they made crepe paper crocuses. These four student nurses are about to tag the public for money to purchase new equipment for the hospital. They chose the Saturday nearest May 12, commemorating the birthday of Florence Nightingale. From L to R they are: Helen Ritchie, Isobel Lamont, Grace Boles, Christine Hutton.

The luxuriously-draped windows of the Rose Room of the Prince Edward Hotel provide an elegant background for this photo of the 1937 class of graduates of the Brandon General Hospital School of Nursing. Five mothers of city graduates are hostesses for the occasion. Standing, from L to R: Nancy Buchanan, Wilma Mitchell, Annabelle Hutton, Muriel Hamlen, Margaret Taylor, Edith Perry, Phyllis James, Margaret McLean, Miss McNally, Miss Christina McLeod, Miss Helen Morrison, Edith McBurney, Margaret Goodwin, Bernice Petz, Eleanor Bray, Nora McCormick, Isabel Campbell, Edith Gould. Seated: Mabel Parrett, Jeanette McLean, Mrs. Goodwin, Mrs. Sopp, Mrs. Parrett, Mrs. Hutton, Mrs. Hamlen, Jean Evans, Martha Sopp.

Family affairs are usually private, but this event deserves public recognition. Mr. and Mrs. Charles H. Durrant are cutting a wedding anniversary cake to celebrate 72 years of married life.

Among the many who came to their home to congratulate them in March of 1949 were Prime Minister Louis St. Laurent and his wife.

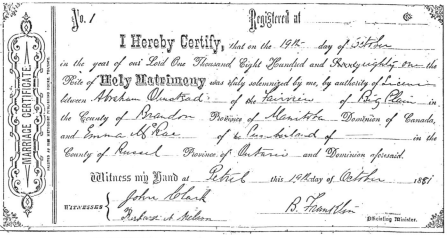

Just a few years after Mr. and Mrs. Durrant were married in England, marriage license number one was issued by Reesor's in the County of Brandon to Abraham Olmstead and Emma McRae.

Mr. and Mrs. Olmstead were celebrating their 69th wedding anniversary when this photo was taken in 1950. They lived in the Carberry district.

Here is a rare photo — some of the first settlers to arrive in the Brandon Hills. The occasion is a christening. From left to right they are: John H. Roddick, Melville Roddick holding son Hawkin, Gertie Roddick (nee McKay), R. F. Roddick, Mrs. Henry Dunbar (nee Mary Roddick), Henry Dunbar and son Alexander, David Roddick and son Ray, Mrs. Phoebe Roddick (nee Foxall), Mrs. Elizabeth Roddick, wife of Rev. George Roddick beside her. In the buggy are Mrs. Fred Harris (nee Georgina Roddick) and Mrs. Robert Dunbar (nee Lena Roddick). The meeting is at the Rev. Roddick's home, and that is his horse and buggy.

Four generations of Mrs. William Evans's family are shown here. Even the baby co-operated by sitting still for this important photo.

If you recall the design of lady Diana Spencer's wedding gown, you will recognize some similarities with this gown worn by Mrs. John Muirhead on her wedding day.

"What's a table richly spread
Without a woman at its head?"
(from an old valentine
in Daly House Museum)

Here is a happy occasion,
although photography techniques
of an earlier era did not seem to
encourage smiles. The ladies are
celebrating the birthdays of Mrs.
Morrison and Mrs. Robert Rae
(70) on October 12, 1912. Going
around the table the guests are:
Mrs. Barrie, Mrs. Berry, Mrs. Kate
McPhayden, Mrs. McKinnon, Mrs.
Wallace (at the head of the table),
Mrs. John McLean, Mrs. Lamont,
Mrs. Morrison, Mrs. Robert
Purdon, Mrs. Robert Rae, the
hostess. Mrs. Wallace has admitted
her age, 85, but the other ladies
aren't telling.

Some of North Brandon's pioneers
have been invited to dinner and
an evening of reminiscing at the
Alex McPhail home, in 1951.
Seated around the table are Dunc
Forsythe, W. G. Buckley, J. A.
Grant, John Clarke, Alex
Anderson, D. G. McKenzie, Ed
Hutchinson, Harvey Richards,
Russell Mansfield, Jack McCallum,
Alex McPhail, Tom Phillips,
William Anderson, Ritchie
McPherson, Jim Nicol, Dan
Webster, Alex Millar.

It was only a two-hour visit but
Brandon went all out to welcome
the Governor-General of Canada,
HRH The Duke of Connaught, the
Duchess, and Princess Patricia
when they visited the city in
October, 1912.

This massive portal, topped
with sheaves of wheat from the
1912 crop, greeted the royal
visitors as they started out on a
motorcade to City Hall. There the
Duke reviewed veterans of earlier
wars — the South African War,
Fenian Raids, and the Northwest
Rebellion.

A few years later on Arbor
Day, a tree was planted on
Victoria Avenue to honour His
Royal Highness, who served
Canada as Governor-General from
1911 to 1916.

The Duke and Duchess of
Connaught and Princess Patricia
call at Brandon College during
their visit to Brandon.

The year 1927 was Canada's Diamond Jubilee, and along with many celebrations that year Brandon received a royal visit. Two future kings, HRH Edward, Prince of Wales, and HRH Prince George, Duke of Kent, are shown here being welcomed by mayor Harry Cater. Stanley Baldwin stands behind Prince George.

Thousands of people watched from every possible vantage point near the CPR depot as the royal guests shook hands with some 250 veterans.

OUR LOYALTY
TO THE
BRITISH CROWN

The coronation of King George VI, May 12, 1937, was the occasion for this expression of loyalty from the Polish Sokol group in Brandon. The float was one of many in the noon-time parade through the city. The day's celebrations ended with a beacon fire on the north hill.

The shadow of war loomed over the world when Brandon received this brief visit from HRH King George VI and Queen Elizabeth on May 24, 1939.

Despite efforts by the City's Mayor Young and MLA George Dinsdale to have a longer visit, only a 20-minute stop at the CPR depot was allowed. Thousands of school children were massed around the depot to try to catch a glimpse of the royal visitors.

HRH Princess Elizabeth, heir to the British throne, and her husband, The Duke of Edinburgh, received a gift from the City of Brandon for their first-born son, Prince Charles. Here is a Trans Canada Airlines attendant receiving this very special parcel from the City Clerk's Office, Brandon.

A letter from Mayor T. Williamson to Her Majesty, dated November 17, 1948, said in part:

"May God be pleased to grant to the new Prince a long life of health and happiness, with a heart of love and devotion to those things which are true and lovely and of good report . . . ."

What was in the parcel? A Rokorol, a piece of nursery furniture invented by Roy Brown, and donated to the City to be sent to the new Prince. This versatile unit can be adjusted to serve as a walker-playpen, a sled, or even as an infant's crib. The inventor's own son, Wayne, is shown in the rocker.

This photo of Her Majesty Queen Elizabeth II escorted by Mayor James Creighton is understandably a highly-treasured memento of the Royal Visit to Brandon in July, 1959. A ten-car motorcade took the distinguished visitors from the Royal Train to the Exhibition Grounds where five thousand school children had an opportunity to greet the Queen and Prince Philip.

The Brandon Roller Rink, built in 1885, was used as an assembly place and concert hall on occasion, as well as for its original recreational purpose. It was here that a Cycling Club was organized that same year. This very early photo shows the Wheat City Lodge lining up for a parade.

ROSSER AVENUE OF THE 12TH JULY, BRANDON, MANITOBA.

Maybe the weather had something to do with it, or maybe it was the white charger, but the year 1905 brought nine special CPR trains full of visitors to Brandon to celebrate the glorious twelfth of July. About 14,000 people converged on Brandon that day. A parade a mile and a half long, led by the traditional white horse and comprised of twenty brass bands and fifty Orange lodges with their banners aloft, marched downtown and on to the Exhibition Grounds.

Here is one section of that parade, in the 700 block of Rosser Avenue.

Rolls and rolls of crepe paper were used to decorate the Olivers' car for the Brandon Fair parade in the summer of 1926. Mr. Borthwick and Mr. George Oliver with his two little girls Isabel and Margaret are pleased with their entry.

Coffee breaks were not part of accepted working conditions some forty years ago. In fact, these workers at the McKenzie Seeds plant have a number of grievances, which have been spelled out on placards they are carrying in this parade down Ninth Street circa March, 1944. Some of the signs said: "one toilet for seventy girls, unfair to labor, poor heating conditions, our cloakroom is a seed bin, drinking cups are seed packets", and so on. The gentleman who appears to be leading the parade, with some apparent reluctance, has been identified as the founder of the firm, Mr. McKenzie.

In more recent times decorated cars became "floats" in the downtown parades. In 1963 the City welcomed visitors to the Brier with a parade, and the Lions were still able to find a roll or two of crepe paper to help gussy up this car.

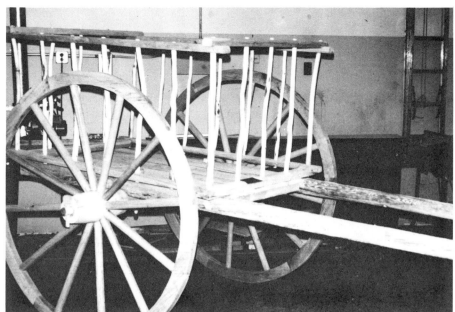

Brandon is hosting the Brier again in '82, and to make the bid for the games, a contingent of local businessmen went to Halifax in the winter of '81.

They did not arrive in a glittery car with Leo atop; they arrived in great humility with this ox cart. And rather than ride it back home, Rick Borotsik presented it to the Mayor of Halifax.

The cart was made in Brandon (it is engraved for all to see) by the Westbran Work Activity Project.

Imagine having 3,000 turn up for a barbecue! That's what happened when Brandon Brier '82 issued a "y'all come" to their Halifax hosts. Jimmy Moffatt didn't bat an eye; he just kept turnin' those little pork patties till Haligonians cried "enough!" Russ Gurr is someplace in this crowd singin' for his supper.

The Bay has come back to Brandon after an absence of 150 years. Brandon House, the Hudson's Bay Company trading post which was located just a few miles downstream from where Brandon is now situated, was closed in 1831. This newer version of the HBC trading post exchanges merchandise for paper or plastic rather than for pelts. The Bay opened its doors March 11, 1981.

Angela Kelman, a recent graduate of Crocus Plains Regional Secondary School and one of Brandon's popular young vocal artists, is appealing to her classmates to sing up for the Prime Minister. Mr. Trudeau was a guest of the three Brandon high schools at a mass rally held at Crocus Plains on February 4, 1981.

The message for Prime Minister Trudeau is clear: "Say NO to Garrison Project." Brandon University students parade in front of Crocus Plains Regional Secondary School where the Prime Minister is addressing a mass meeting of Brandon high school students.

They expected perhaps a couple hundred to turn out for the official opening of Pacific Western Airlines' new service linking Toronto, Calgary, and Vancouver with Brandon. Here is a part of the estimated three thousand that came to see the long-awaited service become a reality on May 31, 1981.

Moments after touching down on the landing strip at Brandon's Municipal Airport, this PWA jet was greeted with a thunderous welcome of cheers and applause as it taxied up to the terminal.

A tour from Iceland paid a visit to Brandon the first week of the opening of Pacific Western service. The visitors are making their way to the terminal where a smorgasbord has been spread out to welcome them.

In 1881 the birth of Brandon city was contingent upon the Canadian Pacific Railway's choice of a location for a divisional point in the Canadian Northwest. In 1981 Brandon's direct air link with major cities in the West and in the East gives promise that we are again on the threshold of an era of vigorous growth. The seeds that promise this growth have not been random "happenings". They have been carefully and persistently planted, and the ensuing growth will be nurtured with diligence and with care.

# Acknowledgements

Countless individuals have generously contributed towards the preparation of this book — people who have loaned photographs, scrapbooks, souvenir brochures and special newspaper editions, magazines and books — and also those who have shared their personal recollections of earlier life in our city and rural areas.

I acknowledge with gratitude the assistance of the following persons as well: Malcolm Jolly, John Keogh, Tom Mitchell and Eva Campbell — members of the Editor's Advisory Committee; Sr. Betty Iris Bartush, Joyce Cooper, David C. Wilson, and Tom Mitchell — colleagues who have contributed to the writing of the text; John Jacobson, Len Sandeman, and the senior Commercial Arts students at Crocus Plains Regional Secondary School for their work on the design; Catherine McLaren and Rebecca Moritz for their dedication to the preparation of the text and the lay-out respectively.

# Photograph Acknowledgements

Agriculture Canada Research Station: Page 4, 84 lower (lo), 113 upper (up), 118 lo, 119, 120 up, 120 centre (ce)
Aidun, Gol: 137 up

Armstrong, Myrtle: 156 up, 172 ce

Bain, Thelma: 31, 116 up
Bass, Mrs. N. G.: 163
Birtles, William: 178 lo, 186 lo, 187 lo
Bjarnason, Linda: 140 up
Blair, Robert: 193 lo
Brandon Fire Department: 12, 105 up, 184 up
Brandon Flying Club: 6, 83 lo, 171 lo
Brandon Lions Club: 136, 196 lo
Brandon School Division Archives: 74 up, 141 lo, 142 up, 177 lo
Brandon Sun: 35 lo, 174 up, 174 lo, 175 up, 175 lo
Brandon University Archives: 69 lo, 70, 71 up, 71 lo, 192 lo
Brown, Ron: 107 lo
Brown, Roy: 39 lo, 153, 194 up, 194 ce
Buga, Bill: 130 lo, 155 up
Burgess, Ken: 29
Butler, Leila: 111 ce

Cairns, Mrs. J. W.: 169 up
Campbell, Eva: 156 ce
Central United Church: 131 lo
Children's Aid Society: 156 lo
Chrest, Nick: 68 lo
Coates, R.: 74 lo, 141 up
Cochrane, Ken: 198 lo, 199 up
Cooper, Joyce: 190 lo
Cosgrove, Grant: 154 up
Creighton, James: 34 lo, 160 lo, 194 lo
Cumming, Muriel: 110 up, 179 lo
Czerkawski, Elsie: 154 lo, 193 ce

Daly House Museum: 6, 8, 14, 22, 26, 27, 28, 33 lo, 34 up, 36, 37, 39 up, 43, 44, 45 lo, 46 lo, 49 lo, 50 up, 53, 54 lo, 55 up, 60, 61 up, 63 lo, 64 lo, 65 up, 65 ce, 67, 72, 73 up, 80 up, 85 up, 85 ce, 86 lo, 89, 96 up, 99 lo, 103 lo, 104, 106 up, 108 up, 109 up, 111 up, 112 lo, 113 ce, 114 up, 115, 117 up, 134 up, 135, 137 lo, 138 up, 149 lo, 151 up, 152 lo, 159, 160 up, 161 up, 162 up, 164, 165, 166, 167 up, 169 lo, 170 lo, 172 lo, 176 lo, 180, 182, 186 ce, 187 up. 190 ce, 195 up.
David Livingstone School: 78 lo

Endall, Florence: 78 up

Flay, Jeanne: 146 lo, 147, 150 lo
Fowell, Cyril: 13

Grant, Jean: 117 lo
Guild, Muriel: 179 up, 180 up

Harrison, Ila: 183 lo, 189 up
Hawkins, Mrs. D. C.: 171 up, 195 ce
Henderson, Fran: 116 lo
Hendzel, Helen: 121 lo
Hickling, R.: 167 ce
Hildebrand, Daisy: 66c, 75 lo
Hockley, Gwen: 24, 134 lo, 152 up
Hughes and Co.: 2, 41 lo, 46 up, 120 lo, 121 up, 121 ce
Isleifson, J.: 199 lo, 200 lo

Knowlton, Betty: 66 up

Lamont, Isobel: 188 up

Lane, Norah: 11, 128 up
Larkins, Arthur E.: 21, 184 lo, 185 up
Leech, C.E.: 82 lo, 83 up
Leech Printing: 77 up, 95 up, 96 lo, 109 up, 128 lo, 130 up, 132, 133 lo, 138 lo, 140 lo, 170 ce, 172 up, 173 lo, 201
Lepard, G.: 129 up

Manitoba Archives: 32, 35 up, 35 ce, 41 up, 45 up, 50 lo, 54 up, 54 ce, 82 up (Foote coll.), 90 lo, 94 up, 107 up, 113 lo, 162 ce, 176 ce, 181
Manitoba Department of Industry and Commerce: 56
Marshall, Barbara: 193 up
McGuinness, Fred: 41 ce, 55 lo, 110 lo, 168 up
McLaren, Catherine: 200 up
McPhail, Mrs. A. P.: 66 lo, 81 up, 86 up, 87 lo, 88 up, 93, 108 lo, 126 lo, 190 up, 191
Moffatt, James: 80 lo, 158 lo
Moore, Clarence: 75 ce, 76 up
Moroz, Peter: 77 lo, 151 lo, 157 ce, 186 up
Morphy, Derek: 150 up

New Era School: 75 up
Nicol, E. B.: 110 ce, 188 lo
Nordin, Henry: 76 lo

Olmstead, Bert: 19 ce, 189 lo
Ostash, Peter: 17
Outhwaite, Muriel: 109 lo

Patmore, Hazel: 118 up, 118 ce
Photography Unlimited: 161 lo
Pottinger, Don: 197
Provincial Archives of British Columbia: 38 up, 58 up
Provincial Exhibition of Manitoba: 7, 51, 52 up, 91, 92, 95 lo, 97 lo, 98, 99 up, 100, 101, 102 lo, 157 lo, 170 up
Public Archives of Canada: 9 (PA 124508), 15 (PA 12338), 33 up (PA 124507), 40 (c 22399), 59 lo (PA 53003), 61 lo (PA 124510), 62 up (PA 124511), 62 lo (PA 124512), 64 up (PA 124509), 81 lo (PA 21586), 114 lo (PA 11485)

Riverheights School: 79 lo
Robertson, Peggy: 1, 73 ce, 122 lo, 183 up
Rowe, Kaye: 125 up
Royal Ontario Museum: 30 ce

St. Matthew's Cathedral: 133 up
Shaw, Isabel: 127, 129 lo, 195 lo
Smart, Mary: 71 ce, 139 lo, 148 lo, 185 ce
Stott, George: 89 ce, 97 up, 108 ce
Stuckey, Lawrence: 18, 38 lo, 42, 47, 48, 49 up, 52 lo, 57 up, 57 lo (Frank Gowan), 59 up, 63 up, 65 lo, 67 lo, 68 up, 69 up, 94 lo, 103 up, 105 lo, 106 lo, 111 lo, 122 up, 123, 124 lo, 131 up, 155 lo, 173 up, 185 lo, 198 up

Thordarson, Kathleen: 125 lo, 145 up
Trotter, Marjorie: 73 lo
Turner, Robert: 151 ce

Vancouver Public Library: 58 lo

Washington, William: 19, 30 lo, 177 up, 178 up
Western Canada Pictorial Index: 10, 23, 30 up, 85 lo, 90 up, 154 ce, 192 up
Williamson, Lil: 102 up
Wilson, David C.: 126 up, 139 up, 143, 144, 148 up

Yeomans, M.A.: 145 lo, 146 up, 149 up, 177 ce

# Some Sources of Information

## BOOKS

Barker, Graham F. *Brandon, A City*. Published by the author, 1971.

Berton, Pierre. *The Great Railway*. McClelland and Stewart, 1972.

Bigelow, Dr. W. *Forceps, Fin and Feather*. D. W. Friesen, 1968.

Brown, Roy. *The Fort Brandon Story*. Tourism Unlimited, 1974.

Brumfield, Kirby. *This Was Wheat Farming*. Superior Publishing Co., 1968.

Coleman, MacDonald. *The Face of Yesterday. The story of Brandon, Manitoba*. Leech Printing, 1957.

Elliott, W.A. *No Drum Went Dead. The story of the Elliott Family Concert Orchestra*. Published privately, 1951.

Kavanagh, Martin. *The Assiniboine Basin. A social study of the discovery, exploration and settlement of Manitoba*. Public Press, 1946.

Liddell, Ken. *I'll Take the Train*. Modern Press, Prairie Books Service, 1966.

MacEwan, Grant. *Power for Prairie Plows*. The Western Producer, 1971.

Mann, Margaret. *The Strike That Wasn't*. Chalk Talk Publishing Co., 1972.

Stone, C.G. and F. Joan Garnett. *Brandon College: A History, 1899 - 1967.*, 1969.

Trotter, Beecham. *A Horseman in the West*. MacMillan, 1925.

Tyman, John Langton. *By Section, Township and Range. Studies in Prairie Settlement*. Assiniboine Historical Society, 1972.

## MISCELLANEOUS MATERIALS

Bjarnason, Carl. *The Brandon School System. A historical survey and ten-year developmental program*, 1962.

*Clark, Leland. Politics in Brandon City, 1899 - 1949.*, 1976.

The Brandon Daily Sun. November 12, 1918; October 30, 1920; 75 Anniversary Issue, 1956; July 14, 1970; September 3, 1970.

# Index to Photographs

# NOTES